In 1994 Trevor Dennis joined the s                   
he is Vice Dean. For nearly 12 ye:
Old Testament Studies at Salisbury
During his time at Salisbury he wrote two books on Old Testament
narratives, *Lo and Behold!* (1991), and *Sarah Laughed* (1994), and
these were later followed by two volumes exploring Old Testament
stories of encounter with God, *Looking God in the Eye* (1998), and
*Face to Face with God* (1999). He is well known to readers of the
Bible Reading Fellowship's *Guidelines* series of Bible notes for his
contributions on Old Testament books. Before going to Salisbury
he was a chaplain at Eton College, and there he began preaching
occasionally through storytelling, a practice he has continued ever
since. SPCK has published five collections of his pieces, *Speaking of
God* (1992), *Imagining God* (1997), *The Three Faces of Christ* (1999),
*Keeping God Company* (2002), and *God Treads Softly Here* (2004).
In 2003 Lion published his children's Bible, but *The Christmas
Stories* is his first book exploring New Testament narratives in detail.
It furnished him with the inspiration for his reflections in the BBC
Radio 4 Christmas Day service in 2006. He makes use of the other
string to his bow by including in it a number of stories and verse
meditations, four of them never published before. He is married to
Caroline, and they have four children and one grandson.

# THE CHRISTMAS STORIES

## Trevor Dennis

First published in Great Britain in 2007

Society for Promoting Christian Knowledge
36 Causton Street
London SW1P 4ST

*British Library Cataloguing-in-Publication Data*
A catalogue record for this book is available from the British Library

ISBN 978–0–281–05848–8

3 5 7 9 10 8 6 4

Typeset by Graphicraft Ltd, Hong Kong
Printed in Great Britain by Ashford Colour Press

Produced on paper from sustainable forests

*For Caroline*
*and for Eleanor, Sarah,*
*Jo and John (and James, when he's a bit older),*
*Tim and Elizabeth*

Salvation to all that will is nigh;
That All, which always is All every where,
Which cannot sinne, and yet all sinnes must beare,
Which cannot die, yet cannot chuse but die,
Loe, faithfull Virgin, yields himselfe to lye
In prison, in thy womb; and though he there
Can take no sinne, nor thou give, yet he'will weare
Taken from thence, flesh, which deaths force may trie.
Ere by the spheares time was created, thou
Wast in his minde, who is thy Sonne, and Brother;
Who thou conceiv'st, conceived; yea thou art now
Thy Makers maker, and thy Fathers mother;
Thou hast light in darke; and shutst in little roome,
Immensity cloistered in thy deare wombe.

*(John Donne, 'Annunciation', from his
cycle of seven sonnets reflecting on
the life of Christ, La Corona.)*

Blessed art thou,
O Christmas Christ,
that thy cradle was so low
that shepherds,
poorest and simplest of earthly folk,
could yet kneel beside it,
and look level-eyed into the face of God.

(Anon.)

# Contents

# Acknowledgements

The translation of the Matthean and Lukan passages discussed in the book is Trevor Dennis' own. In all other cases, where explicit acknowledgement is not made in the text, the translation is taken from the *New Revised Standard Version of the Bible* © 1989.

I would like to thank my colleagues at Chester Cathedral for allowing me to take a three-month sabbatical, and for covering for me in my absence. Without that period of leave, I would not have started on the book, let alone finished it.

Alison Barr, Senior Editor at SPCK, set me on the road towards writing it by asking me, 'Why don't you consider writing something on the New Testament of the kind you have written on the Old?' I am most grateful to her for that prompting, and for all the encouragement she has given me since then, from the time when I submitted a formal proposal to SPCK through to publication. SPCK has been very good to me over the years, and I would also like to record my thanks to other members of the SPCK team including Sally Green, Monica Capoferri, and Trisha Dale, the copy-editor.

As always, my greatest debt is to my wife and family. This book is dedicated to them.

# 1

## Nativity plays and all that

I guess all or most of us have memories of nativity plays. Many years ago our eldest daughter, Eleanor, played the part of a shepherd in a nativity play at her local playgroup. Unfortunately, her younger sister, Sarah, upstaged her. She didn't mean to. She was not much over a year old at the time. She was too young to be a member of the playgroup, of course, but its leaders wanted to include as many younger siblings as possible (as if they weren't running a big enough risk as it was!). So Sarah was a sheep. A good part for her to play, you might have thought, since she was at the crawling stage, and therefore took naturally to being on all fours. Eleanor had the obligatory tea towel on her head, and Sarah was covered in a white woolly shawl. Very suitable for a sheep, we thought. The trouble was there were no sheepdogs in the cast, to keep her in order. She kept on crawling off, and I'm afraid became rather a distraction for everybody, as Caroline, my wife, continually had to rescue her and point her back in the right direction.

A few years later, when Sarah was at infants' school, we went to another nativity play. This time she played the part of Mary, and with remarkable assurance for one so young sang the first verse of 'Away in a manger' as a solo. There was hardly a dry eye in the place, and I will never forget it. She still sings, does Sarah.

In another school, in another town, our third daughter, Jo, played her part in a nativity play. But it was her best friend I remember most. Aged eight, Jemma had stage presence. She didn't know it, but she did. She was the angel Gabriel, and what I recall above all else was her hands. She stood behind Mary and Joseph and the baby Jesus in her long white robe, and stretched up her arms above them in a gesture of blessing

1

and protection. Her hands were so small! I remember thinking at the time that a bigger person could not communicate what she was expressing. The body language would be different, the hands simply too big. I have never forgotten that moment, either.

In Chester Cathedral, at the crib service on Christmas Eve 2005, we had a real baby. No donkey, no camels, but at least we had a real baby. The children of the Sunday school provided the cast. A relative of one of the mums had recently had a baby. And so it was, that after Mary and Joseph had taken their places beside the crib and the time for 'the birth' arrived, the mother of the baby slipped on to the platform, placed her child carefully in the crib, and scuttled off again as inconspicuously as she could. It was marvellous to behold. The baby was well fed and didn't murmur. It lay there for the rest of the play, as good as gold, remaining undisturbed when the youngest of the shepherds, just two, couldn't restrain himself from showing her his teddy. Yes, the baby Jesus that day was a girl.

Sometimes, of course, children who are older than one or two decide to do things their own way. Mary and Joseph arrive at Bethlehem, and knock on the door of the inn to be met by an innkeeper who instead of saying, 'No room here, sorry', smiles and says, 'Of course, come in. Which room would you like?' and the teachers put their hands over their eyes and shake their heads, while Mary and Joseph stand there, not knowing what to do next. Pat Alexander, in her book, *Star of Wonder*, gives us a particularly poignant version of this 'amendment' to the story. It relates to a school in the Midwest of the United States and a nine-year-old boy called Wallace Purling. Wallace was a great supporter of the underdog. He himself had learning difficulties. But he knew his part well. Joseph knocked loudly on the inn door.

Wallace, the innkeeper, opened it wide. 'What do you want?' he asked.

'My wife is expecting a baby,' said Joseph. 'Do you have a room where she can bring him to birth, and where we can put the baby to sleep?'

'No room, sorry,' said Wallace. 'Try next door.' So far so good; word perfect.

Mary and Joseph looked very sad, just as they had been taught. 'But please can we come in?'

'Sorry, no room,' replied Wallace.

'Please,' said Joseph, looking and sounding even sadder.

A tear came into Wallace's eye. He looked at Mary and Joseph. 'You can have my room, if you like.'

A friend of my daughter Eleanor once said to her, 'I only know one story in the Bible: Noah and the whale.' I would guess that wasn't true. If pressed, she would probably have admitted she knew the stories of the journey to Bethlehem and the angels and shepherds and kings. In our society, when the joke is already very old about the man who goes into the jeweller's shop to buy a cross on a chain for his wife and is asked by the assistant, 'Do you want a plain one, or one with a little man on it?', and when some think they only know about Jonah and the whale, the nativity play exercises a vital role in keeping countless people in touch with a key part of the tale the Bible has to tell. Indeed, even for many of us churchgoing Christians, it continues to help shape our understanding of what we call 'the Christmas story', that and carols and carol services, half-remembered children's Bibles, Christmas cards, paintings, stained glass windows, sculptures, films and sermons.

Yet, even those of us who have been going to church for years may not realize quite how far the nativity play and the rest have taken us from the Bible itself. For a start, there is not one, but two Christmas stories in the Bible, and their differences outweigh their similarities.

Matthew's story is a dark tale, or rather, a tale of light shining in fearful darkness. Jesus is born into a dangerous world, where a young girl who becomes pregnant before her time must hide behind her mother's skirts, when the news is told to her father, and where she, her child and her whole family risk being overwhelmed by disgrace. Matthew begins to explore that disgrace, and tells of how the Holy Spirit of God will turn it to extravagant hope. Yet the danger does not end there, for Jesus is born too close to the centre of power in Jerusalem and especially to Herod, and the news of his birth is spread by magi who seem more skilled at reading stars than politics. They succeed in causing both general and particular paranoia, and the result, after they have found the child Jesus and returned home, is a most terrible massacre of babies and infants, from which Jesus escapes, but then, with Mary and Joseph, at once becomes a refugee in a country tainted by its own ancient oppression.

Matthew's fragile Jesus, born at home in Bethlehem, with the women of the family and the neighbouring houses no doubt in attendance, is a candle in a dark world, where the breeze of human frailty and the storm of men's concern for their power and their honour threaten to blow it out, and nearly succeed.

The nativity play rarely draws on Matthew, except on his story of the magi, but then those figures are turned into wise men and from there into kings, while the fear they engender in the hearts of Herod and the inhabitants of Jerusalem, and the terrible mayhem of the slaughter that follows in their wake, are generally left aside.

'The Christmas story', as we know it, has much more to do with Luke's version, which is full of the light and joy we wish to find in the feast of Christmas. Clouds do pass over Luke's Christmas sky: Zechariah, the father of John the Baptist, whose birth precedes that of Jesus (but without featuring in most of our plays and carols), becomes temporarily mute and deaf; Mary's initial fear and bewilderment in her annunciation scene is real enough, while for the birth she has to travel at least 85 miles because of an order of the Roman emperor; in her famous song we call the Magnificat she makes mention of the 'humiliation' of hers which God has overcome; and in the penultimate scene Simeon speaks of the sword that will pierce her soul, and of the opposition her son one day will meet. Yet these details are not typical, and do not determine the general tone. In Luke there is no threat to Mary's relationship with Joseph; there are no magi blundering about Jerusalem; there is no Herod, either. Though Augustus in distant Rome makes life somewhat precarious for a few days, he poses no threat after that. He sends no soldiers, and there is no slaughter, no flight, no living as refugees in Egypt. Nor, if we understand Luke aright, is there an inn from which Mary and Joseph are turned away, let alone a filthy stable for the birth. Instead there are songs of thanksgiving and joy, a baby safely laid in a manger, angels dancing and singing all over heaven, and shepherds running through the dark to find warm belonging. The whole story, this small part of the tale Luke tells in his Gospel and continues in Acts, ends where it begins, in the temple in Jerusalem, but the temple authorities who later will play such a significant role in Jesus' arrest and execution are either nowhere to be seen, or else are simply intrigued by what they see or hear.

We will spend the bulk of our time in the rest of this book examining these two Christmas stories, Matthew's first, then Luke's, trying to read them as if we were doing so for the first time. We will put out of our minds the nativity plays and the carols, wonderful though they may be. We will also free our minds of any Christian doctrine that might be there. We are told that both Matthew and Luke speak of a virgin birth, and indeed we often hear it said that such an understanding is necessary, even central to the Christian faith. We will approach Matthew and Luke with an open and a questioning mind, curious to see what they really do say on the matter, and whether that is clear and unambiguous.

We will endeavour to take with full seriousness the nature of the material we will be handling. That means recognizing it as storytelling, as art. Too often, in sermons, television or radio discussion, or in film, the assumption is made that Matthew or Luke simply and straightforwardly recorded events as they happened, or faithfully handed on the transcripts of eyewitnesses who came before them. That assumption is false. At the beginning of the film *Ben-Hur*, first shown in 1959, the star of Matthew's magi story is shown moving visibly across the night sky, until it stops above the village of Bethlehem and then sends down a searchlight beam hitting the place where the baby Jesus lies. This reduces Matthew's wonderful, many-layered story to bathos. Far from showing us how true his story must be, it makes it ridiculous.

Equally, we will not characterize the stories of Jesus' birth as 'mere' legends, or myths. Even within biblical scholarship, which should know a lot better, we sometimes find the opening chapters of Matthew's and Luke's Gospels dismissed as

5

having nothing to tell us about the 'real' Jesus of Nazareth, and as being of less value than the material that does. Outside academia, also, they are too often ignored, or even despised as fanciful, as clearly 'not true', as suitable for young children, perhaps, and for turning into nice nativity plays, but not worthy of mature consideration.

Instead, we will try to pay full heed to the artistry, the creativity, the imaginations of Matthew and Luke, knowing that poetic stories like theirs, so full of symbolism and so rich with meaning, can take us far nearer truth and far deeper into the heart of God than any mechanical reporting of events. If they have legendary qualities, then legends can have extraordinary power over our imaginations. If we could rightly call them myths, then such tales are designed to be the ones we live by, and are of all kinds of story the most significant.

At two points we will pause to offer a few reflections of our own, which will bring our own faith, experience and imagination to bear on the birth stories, and provide a different kind of commentary.

# 2

# *What of Paul, Mark and John?*

There is not one, but two Christmas stories in the New Testament. But there are only two. The Gospels are not the New Testament's earliest works. Those are the letters of Paul, but though he mentions Jesus' birth several times, his concern seems to be with the mere fact of its occurrence. He tells no stories about it. Whether he did in his initial preaching and teaching, when he first established and nurtured the Christian communities, we do not know. In his first letter to the Christians at Corinth he writes, 'I decided to know nothing among you except Jesus Christ, and him crucified,' (1 Corinthians 2.2). That is not entirely true, of course, since everything Paul writes is informed by the resurrection of Jesus and by his own encounter with the crucified *and risen* Christ. Nor can we be clear what Paul has in mind when he says, 'I decided to know nothing among you except *Jesus Christ.*' How much of what we know about Jesus from the Gospels is contained in that phrase 'Jesus Christ'? It is impossible to be certain, but the fact remains that in all his letters Paul is pre-occupied with Jesus' death and resurrection, and appears to have no interest in the circumstances of his birth. Attempts have been made by some to find support in Paul for the doctrine of the virgin birth, but only those who think that such a belief is essential to the Christian faith and therefore must have been promulgated by him will find them convincing.

There are only two Christmas stories, or rather only two series of stories about the birth of Jesus in the New Testament. Paul, or no Paul, we might have expected four, because, of course, there are four Gospels. Yet there is nothing at all about the birth of Jesus in either Mark, or John, almost certainly the first and the last of the Gospels to be written.

The beginning of Mark's Gospel is abrupt and awkward:

> The beginning of the Gospel of Jesus Christ. (1.1) As it is written in the prophet Isaiah, 'See, I am sending my messenger ahead of you, who will prepare your way; the voice of one crying out in the wilderness: "Prepare the way of the Lord, make his paths straight." '  (1.2–3)

There are two main difficulties with this: first, how are we to understand verse 1, and second, how can Mark launch straight into a biblical quotation without introducing it properly? He refers the lines of Isaiah to John the Baptist and his preaching in the desert. Matthew and Luke do the same, but bring John onto the stage first: 'In those days,' says Matthew,

> John the Baptist appeared in the wilderness of Judea, proclaiming, 'Repent, for the kingdom of God has come near.' This is the one of whom the prophet Isaiah spoke when he said, 'The voice of one crying in the wilderness.'
> (Matthew 3.1–3a)

Luke has:

> In the fifteenth year of the reign of Emperor Tiberius . . . the word of the Lord came to John son of Zechariah in the wilderness. He went into all the region around the Jordan, proclaiming a baptism of repentance for the forgiveness of sins, as it is written in the book of the words of the prophet Isaiah, 'The voice of one crying out in the wilderness.'  (Luke 3.1–4a)

N. Clayton Croy has written at length about the beginning of Mark in his book *The Mutilation of Mark's Gospel*, and concludes that verse 1 is most likely a marker inserted by a second-century scribe who was copying Mark, designed simply to signal the start of a new work: 'Here begins the book of the Gospel of Mark.' As for the Isaiah quotation, he suggests the original copy of the Gospel got damaged at an early date, and that there is something missing. He thinks it likely that Mark originally introduced us to John the Baptist first, in the way Matthew and Luke do. He does not believe, however, that anything more is lost, or that Mark's Gospel once had its own series of stories of the birth of Jesus. The signs are, he says, that when Jesus comes on the scene in 1.9, he is being mentioned for the first time.

Of one thing we can be quite sure: in the Gospel of Mark as we have it, there are no stories of Jesus' birth. There is no annunciation scene; there are no angels, no magi, no shepherds. There may, however, be one veiled reference to the circumstances of the birth.

> [Jesus] came to his home town, and his disciples followed him. On the sabbath he began to teach in the synagogue, and many who heard him were astounded. They said, 'Where did this man get all this? What is this wisdom that has been given to him? What deeds of power are being done by his hands! Is not this the carpenter, the son of Mary and brother of James and Joses and Judas and Simon, and are not his sisters here with us?' And they simply could not take him.
>
> (6.1–3; the translation of the final sentence is my own)

We cannot be sure why Mark has the people refer to Jesus as 'son of Mary'. Given the culture of the times, it is a peculiar description. People were invariably referred to by reference to their father. It may be that Joseph was dead, and Mark knew that, and knew the locals would know that. But it may be Mark's villagers mean that Jesus is illegitimate, and that that, and not just their familiarity with him, explains their amazement and their resistance. Their prejudice blinds them, and prevents them from recognizing the significance of what is happening in front of their eyes. That, at least, is a possible interpretation, and some would argue a probable one.

This is the only time in his whole Gospel that Mark tells us Mary's name. Yet there is one other passage in which she appears, and another which implies her presence:

> [Jesus] went home; and the crowd came together again, so that they could not even eat. When his family heard it, they went out to restrain him, for people were saying, 'He has gone out of his mind.' And the scribes who came down from Jerusalem said, 'He has Beelzebul, and by the

ruler of the demons he casts out demons' . . . Then his mother and his brothers came; and standing outside, they sent to him and called him. A crowd was sitting around him; and they said to him, 'Your mother and your brothers and sisters are outside, asking for you.' And he replied, 'Who are my mother and my brothers?' And looking at those who sat around him, he said, 'Here are my mothers and my brothers! Whoever does the will of God is my brother and sister and mother.'

(3.19b–22, 31–35)

We must take great care in our assessment of this passage. To our ears its Jesus can sound intolerably harsh. Did Jesus really treat his mother and brothers and sisters like that? We have to remind ourselves that Mark is not a recorder of events, let alone of dialogue, but a creative artist, albeit one working with a living tradition. His Gospel, like the other three, has its eye fixed on Jesus at every turn. He is not interested in anyone else, except in so far as they relate to Jesus, or throw light on who he is, or on the significance of his life and work. Nor is he writing for his own benefit, but for Christian communities living a few decades after Jesus' death, who have their own concerns and are facing their own dilemmas. Some find themselves torn between the authority of parents, particularly fathers, and that of the Christian community to which they belong, or the authority of the risen Christ they seek to follow. In the light of other passages in his Gospel we can suggest that what Mark is saying to such people is this: 'It is not easy. Jesus' closest followers found it extremely hard to understand him and to stay with him during his lifetime. His own family disowned him. You have hard choices in front of you. But you belong to the larger family of God now, the family that owns God as its Father, the family that does not recognize the authority of earthly fathers (nor of mothers, if no father is around, nor of brothers), but puts a child at the centre, a child at the head, and turns everything upside down. It is here, in this larger family that you have found and will continue to find the love and the mercy of God. As a member of this new family you belong to God's circle. To take your place here, to continue to occupy your place here, you may have to renounce the ties of blood.'

Yet might that difficult scene in Mark 3 reflect something of the reality of Jesus' situation and the difficulties *he* had to face? We cannot be sure, but we notice again that Mark makes no mention of Jesus' human father. Indeed, we will not find one anywhere in his Gospel, and the name of Joseph never appears. Had Joseph died when Jesus was young? Or had he abandoned Mary and her children? Did Jesus grow up in Galilee as a fatherless child? (Luke has a story about Mary and Joseph going with Jesus to the temple in Jerusalem when he is 12, but many scholars do not regard that as historical.) Remembering the description of him in Mark 6.3 as 'the son of Mary', might we suggest that he, unlike his brothers and sisters, was known not to have been Joseph's child? If those last two suggestions are correct, then Jesus' position in his society was indeed precarious. He would not have been regarded by his fellow Jews as a 'son of Abraham', or as a member of the people of God. He would not have been able to marry a 'daughter of Abraham', a legitimate daughter of a Jewish family. In the temple at Jerusalem, he would not have been allowed further than the Court of the Gentiles. In the thinking and practice of the temple authorities, his birth would have put him at a distance from God. It would also have placed him among people who were on the edge of his society, vulnerable, open to exploitation and often exploited, with no place where they could securely belong, and often poor and despised. If we look at the figure of the adult Jesus in any of the four Gospels, that is precisely where we find him. Might his starting a new family among those who shared his own homelessness or were prepared to journey with him to an uncertain destination, might his delighting in his Father God, might his giving his friends a sense of profound belonging and a new dignity as God's beloved children, might all that have stemmed in part from his own childhood, growing up in Galilee as a fatherless child, despised as illegitimate? The New Testament scholar Andries van Aarde thinks so, and argues his case at length in his book, *Fatherless in Galilee: Jesus as Child of God*, (2001).

When we come to the birth stories in Matthew and Luke, we must avoid manipulating them to fit this picture, yet neither must we forget it. It may be that it will put some of their details into perspective, and bring a new sense, as well as a new poignancy to their stories.

The notion that Jesus was illegitimate, or was thought by some to be so, is closest to the surface in John's Gospel.

> Then Jesus said to the Jews who had believed in him, 'If you continue in my word, you are truly my disciples; and you will know the truth, and the truth will make you free.' They answered him, 'We are descendants of Abraham and have never been slaves to anyone. What do you mean by saying, "You will be made free"?'
>
> Jesus answered them '. . . I know that you are descendants of Abraham; yet you look for an opportunity to kill me, because there is no place in you for my word. I declare what I have seen in the Father's presence; as for you, you should do what you have heard from the Father.'
>
> They answered him, 'Abraham is our father.' Jesus said to them, 'If you were Abraham's children, you would be doing what Abraham did, but now you are trying to kill me, a man who has told you the truth that I heard from God. This is not what Abraham did. You are indeed doing what your father does.' They said to him, '*We* are not illegitimate children; we have one father, God himself.' Jesus said to them, 'If God were your Father, you would love me, for I came from God and now I am here. I did not come on my own, but he sent me.'    (8.31–34, 37–42)

I have italicized the 'we' of the penultimate verse, because in the original Greek of John's text it is plainly emphatic. The whole passage has John's fingerprints all over it. Only in John's Gospel does Jesus speak like this. We hear *John's* voice here. And yet we also hear the voices of people who despise Jesus as illegitimate: 'We are not illegitimate, Jesus, but *you* are.' That is the clear implication of the emphatic 'we' in the Greek. The passage may be of John's making, but he has not composed it out of thin air. Presumably he knew of those who claimed that Jesus was illegitimate. He did not make that up. So what are we to make of it? Throw it aside as a wicked slur, cast by those out for Jesus' blood and quite without foundation? Well, we notice that Jesus in this passage does not deny the charge. Instead, he claims that God is his Father, and that is what matters; he comes from God, trailing God's authority, and that overrides all other considerations. It is almost as if he is saying, 'Yes, I may be illegitimate, but that is of no consequence.'

John's Jesus does not defend himself against the charge of illegitimacy by claiming he had a miraculous birth of a virgin mother. That is not what 'having God as his Father' and 'coming from God' mean. In his famous Prologue, the passage that is read as the last lesson in the traditional Nine Lessons and Carols at Christmas, John instead claims that Jesus existed from the beginning of the world as the mind of God, and then 'became flesh and lived among us' (1.14). Nowhere in that passage, nor anywhere else in his Gospel, does John suggest that Jesus' birth took place through anything other than the normal means of conception.

John tells no stories of Jesus' birth. His Prologue stands in their place. After it is ended, he moves straight into the story of John the Baptist's preaching in the desert and his meeting with the adult Jesus. Yet before we move on ourselves, we should remind ourselves of how the Prologue begins: 'In the beginning was the Word, and the Word was with God, and the Word was God' (1.1).

Near the end of his Gospel, John tells of Thomas being overwhelmed by an encounter with the risen Jesus. He looks at him and says, 'My Lord and my God!' (20.28). Thus John begins and ends his Gospel with bold speech, speaking of Jesus as God, saying that in Jesus we hear the voice of God, in Jesus we see the wounded figure of God. Such daring language is another thing we need to remember when we enter Matthew's and Luke's stories of the birth of Jesus, and when we offer reflections of our own.

But before we do that, let us see what John has to say of Mary. In fact, he does not call her by her name, but marks her as 'the mother of Jesus'. She appears only twice on the stage of his narrative. But what significant appearances those are! She plays a crucial role in the story of the wedding at Cana in John 2.1–11, the first of Jesus' 'signs', as John calls them, the acts that reveal the secret of who he is. And the very next verse after the wedding story has this: 'After this he went down to Capernaum with his mother, his brothers, and his disciples; and they remained there a few days' (2.12).

The tensions that appear in Mark 3 are nowhere to be seen. In the Prologue John writes, 'He came to what was his own, and his own people did not accept him' (1.11). Jesus' family are not among those who reject him. John 2.12 makes that plain, and the account of Jesus' crucifixion makes it even clearer. In Chester Cathedral, where I work, there is a carving of the crucified Christ mounted on the choir screen. He is flanked by two figures, 'the disciple whom Jesus loved' and his mother. That image, so common in Christian churches worldwide, and so beloved of artists down the centuries, is found only in John. Only he places Jesus' mother among the women at Golgotha. Only he places her 'near the cross', able to hear what Jesus is saying. Mark, Matthew and Luke all put the women who are there 'looking on from a distance', or standing 'at a distance', kept there, no doubt, by the Roman soldiers in charge of the execution. Yet John goes further, much further still: 'When Jesus saw his mother and the disciple whom he loved standing beside her, he said to his mother, "Woman, here is your son." Then he said to the disciple, "Here is your mother." And from that hour', John comments, 'the disciple took her into his own home' (19.26–27).

This is far more than an act of compassion designed to make sure Mary is looked after in her grief and her old age. As many have commented, this, for John, is the moment of the founding of the Church. A new family, a new household is established at the point of Jesus' death, formed to carry on and extend his work. And the founding members of that new family, if we can call them that, are his mother, signifying the ideal female disciple, and 'the beloved disciple', signifying the ideal male disciple (notice John puts Mary first).

All the multitude of images of Mary's grief, in icon, painting, sculpture, play and film draw upon that story of John's. And yet we might well say that Mark takes us deeper into her hurt and her pain. For he replaces a few hours of agony with years of bewilderment and seeming rejection. In Mark 3, Mary is presented as an outsider. She and her other children are left out, left out of the story, left out of the circle of grace. Jesus will tell those within that circle, 'Many who are first will be last, and the last will be first' (Mark 10.31). Mary, it seems, is one of the first who are now last. Already vulnerable as a woman without a husband, but at least having sons and daughters who can look after her, she finds her firstborn son denies her any authority within the family. The old ties of kinship, the clan and the blood family are broken apart by Jesus, and a new dream, a new vision, a new reality, a new family are put in their place. But Mary is not part of the dream. Her son has formed a new family of outsiders, in which she has no part.

Does Mary come in from the cold? In one obvious and significant sense she does. In its own telling and retelling of Jesus' story down the centuries the Church has chosen to ignore Mark's portrayal of her. In teaching, preaching and art, it has overlaid it with the pictures of her created by Luke and John, and Matthew, too, and overlapped it so completely, that it cannot be seen at all. Even to Christians who are familiar with the Bible and who are committed members of the Church, it can come as a shock to hear what Mark has done.

But was he right? Was that how it was? We cannot be sure. And yet we do know that not all the members of Jesus' family remained on the outside. Paul in his first letter to the Christians at Corinth speaks of the risen Christ appearing to James (1 Corinthians 15.7), and it is clear from his letter to the Galatians that he means 'James, the Lord's brother' (see 1.19). He there calls him and Cephas, or Peter, and John 'pillars' (2.9). He could hardly give them a more exalted title, for 'pillars' was a description that Jews sometimes gave Abraham, Isaac and Jacob, the founders of their faith. In the book of Acts, Luke also gives a significant role to James as one of the leaders, perhaps *the* leader of the Jerusalem Church (see 12.17; 15.13; 21.18).

And most intriguingly Luke has this near the beginning of Acts, when he is describing the community of Jesus' followers between ascension and Pentecost:

> They returned to Jerusalem from the mount called Olivet . . . When they had entered the city, they went to the room upstairs where they were staying, Peter, and John, and James, and Andrew, Philip and Thomas, Bartholomew and Matthew, James son of Alphaeus, and Simon the Zealot, and Judas son of James. All these were constantly devoting themselves to prayer, together with certain women, *including Mary the mother of Jesus*, as well as his brothers.          (1.12a, 13–14; the italics are mine)

His mention of Mary is both fascinating and frustrating. For what became of her after that? Luke does not tell us. He makes no further mention of her. Yet there she is, at the point where the second part of Luke's story begins, right at the heart of things, as she is at the start of his Gospel.

Luke leaves us with a Mary who has come home.

16

# 3

## *Not just a list of names*

Matthew prefaces his story of the birth of Jesus with a list of names, marking Jesus' origins. Neither Mark nor John has need of such a thing in their Gospels. Luke does, though he puts his genealogy the far side of the stories surrounding the birth, leaving it, indeed, till after the stories of John the Baptist and Jesus' baptism, inserting it at 3.23–38. Matthew's very first verse is this, 'The book of the origin of Jesus Christ, son of David, son of Abraham,' and he then continues with his long list of names, dividing them into three sections: the first begins with 'Abraham was the father of Isaac,' and ends with 'Jesse the father of David the king'; the second begins, 'David was the father of Solomon by the wife of Uriah,' and ends with 'and Josiah the father of Jechoniah and his brothers, at the time of the exile to Babylon'; the third opens with 'After the exile to Babylon Jechoniah was the father of Salathiel,' and closes with 'Jacob was the father of Joseph the husband of Mary, from whom Jesus was born who is called Christ' (1.1–16).

Matthew's and Luke's two lists do not tally with one another. They largely agree between Abraham and David, but thereafter they go their almost entirely separate ways. They do not even agree who was the father of Joseph, Mary's husband. And Luke goes further back than Matthew, concluding with 'son of Adam, son of God' (3.38b). So Matthew in two ways gives greater prominence to Abraham than Luke: he traces Jesus' ancestry back to Abraham and stops there, and he singles out Abraham together with David at the very beginning, in the opening verse of his Gospel.

There is little doubt why he should draw attention to David. He was celebrated as the greatest king the Jews had ever had, and they believed the Messiah so many longed for would be David's descendant. As we have already seen, Matthew closes his list of names with the words 'Jesus who was called Christ'. 'Christ', or *Christos* in the Greek, is a translation of the Hebrew word 'Messiah'. They both mean 'anointed one'.

Yet why should Matthew go out of his way to draw such attention to Abraham? Was it because he wished to emphasize at the start that Jesus was 'a true child of Abraham'? Was it because some were claiming he wasn't? Was it because Matthew also, besides Mark and John, knew of the charge that Jesus was illegitimate? In the last chapter we spelled out some of the consequences of illegitimacy in the society in which Jesus lived. Among them was the refusal to recognize such children as sons or daughters of Abraham. Certainly, when we come to the next passage, the story of Mary's unexpected pregnancy, Matthew's emphasis will be on the disgrace that threatens to engulf it and sweep Joseph and Mary away, and he himself does not believe Joseph was Jesus' father. That is already clear from the way he ends his list of names. He breaks the pattern he has maintained throughout. As we have seen, he does not write, 'Jacob was the father of Joseph, and Joseph was the father of Jesus.' Instead, Joseph is called 'the husband of Mary, from whom Jesus was born'. Enough said.

Then there are the four women in Matthew's list, five including Mary herself. Luke's list has none, not even Mary, but Matthew's has five. One has already appeared in our quotations of the text, Bathsheba, 'the wife of Uriah'. Matthew does not give her name. His Greek even lacks the word for wife. Translated entirely literally, it reads, 'David fathered Solomon from the [feminine version of the direct article] of Uriah.' It is perfectly good Greek, which we might regret, but which Matthew would have taken for granted. We know the woman's name, because of the stories about her in 2 Samuel and 1 Kings. The first of those and the most poignant is in 2 Samuel 11. David sees her while she is bathing and, consumed with lust, sends for her and has sex with her. She becomes pregnant and bravely sends word to the king. He then gets rid of her husband Uriah, and takes her as his queen. The child she brings to birth dies in infancy, but her second son

Solomon eventually becomes David's successor. Scholars are divided on the subject of whether the story in 2 Samuel 11 allows us to say Bathsheba is raped. The writing is sparse, subtle and extremely sophisticated. It does not tell us what to think, but leaves us free to make up our own minds. I myself believe it leaves the question open, but allows us, indeed invites us to consider David's act as rape.

The other three women are Tamar, Rahab and Ruth. Many of the men named in Matthew's list are complete unknowns, but not so the women: they all have their stories in the tradition, carefully preserved in the Hebrew Scriptures, in what Christians commonly call the Old Testament. Ruth has a whole book, admittedly one of the shorter ones, dedicated to her.

Tamar's story appears in Genesis 38, and to say it is colourful is an understatement. Its theology is frankly appalling. It begins with Judah fathering three sons: Er, Onan and Shelah. When Er reaches the age for marriage, Judah arranges for him to marry Tamar. But Er is a 'wicked' man and, so the story goes, the Lord kills him as a result. Following the custom of the times, Judah gives Tamar to his second son, telling Onan to have children by her to keep the name and the memory of his brother alive. Onan, however, is having none of it. The sooner his brother is forgotten the better. So each time he has intercourse with Tamar he practises *coitus interruptus*. That enrages the Lord, who puts him to death also. So then it should be Shelah's turn, at least when he grows up a bit, but Judah is afraid of losing him as well and, when the time comes for the marriage, it does not happen. Tamar is left languishing at home as a widow, still childless. Yet she is a woman of spirit and initiative. She takes matters into her own hands. She has no power, no authority in the family. They belong to Judah. So she has to resort to a trick. When her father-in-law and a friend take their sheep and goats off to the southern hill country for the shearing, she meets them on the road, veiled, disguised as a prostitute. Judah takes an interest, and the bargaining over the price begins. Judah promises to give her a kid from his flocks, but the clever Tamar asks for a deposit: his seal, the cord on which it hangs round his neck, and his staff. They have sex, Judah goes on his way, and Tamar then removes her veil and puts on again the familiar clothes of her widowhood. At long last she is pregnant, but the story is not yet at an end. Judah sends his friend to deliver the kid, but of course he cannot find 'the prostitute' who was hired, and the local people tell him, 'No prostitute has been here.' The two men are bewildered, but think no more about it, until three months later Judah is told Tamar has been 'playing the whore' and that she is pregnant as a result. He pronounces hasty and most fearful judgement, ordering her to be burned, but when someone goes to fetch her, she tells them to show the seal, the cord and the staff to her father-in-law, and say it was their owner who made her pregnant. So the game is up, and thankfully Judah at once gives Tamar due credit and admits he was in the wrong: 'She is more in the right than I, since I did not give her to my son Shelah' (38.26). Tamar safely gives birth to twins, and bows out of the narrative.

Rahab makes her appearance in the book of Joshua, in the stories preceding the destruction of Jericho. She is a prostitute, a real one, living on the very edge of the town, her house built into its defensive walls. When Joshua sends two spies into Jericho to get the lie of the land, they take lodging in Rahab's house, 'and spend the night there'. But the king's own spies have also been busy. They come to the house demanding Rahab bring the men out. Quickly she hides the Israelites on the roof and then tells the men at the door that they have come too late. Yes, the men did come to her, but she does not know where they came from and they left the city just before dark. 'Pursue them quickly', she says, 'for you can overtake them' (Joshua 2.5). The king's men gallop off towards the Jordan, while Rahab throws a rope out of her window, so the Israelite spies can escape down the walls. When four chapters later the city is captured and its population slaughtered, Rahab and her relatives are the only ones to be spared.

Ruth's is a love story, the most beautiful in the entire Bible. But it is not without its dangers, and in many ways it exposes the vulnerability that was part of so many women's lives. It is set a few decades before King David. A woman from Bethlehem, Naomi, returns to the village with her foreign, widowed, daughter-in-law, Ruth. In order for them to survive there, Ruth must find a husband – Naomi's is long dead and she is too old to hope for another. A local farmer, Boaz, is unusually kind to her, and that gives Naomi an idea. She tells Ruth to dress herself up in her best clothes, go down to the place where Boaz is overseeing the threshing of his crops, wait till he lies down to sleep, take off her clothes (that is how Ruth 3.4b should probably be translated) and lie down beside him. 'He will tell you what to do,' says Naomi (3.4c). Throughout her story Ruth is her own woman, and now when it comes to it, she tells Boaz what to do: 'Spread your cloak over your servant', she says, 'for you are next-of-kin' (3.9). That is more than an invitation to protect her from the night's cold. It amounts to a proposal of marriage. That is clear from her reminding Boaz that he is next-of-kin, not to her, of course, but to Naomi, and therefore under obligation to help the woman and accept responsibility for her daughter-in-law. If he does 'spread his cloak' over Ruth, then he will be committing himself to becoming her protector, and that means to being her husband. It is a highly risky strategy, but it works like a dream, and leads to one of the happiest endings in all Scripture. Ruth and Boaz marry, and Ruth has a son who turns out to be the grandfather of David.

Why does Matthew choose to include these women in his list of names? Why these women in particular, and not the matriarchs of Israel – Sarah, Rebekah, Rachel and Leah – or the mother of David (the biblical tradition does not make clear who she was, but surely Matthew would have been able to come up with a name from somewhere)? Matthew himself does not tell us. He leaves it to us to pick up the clues.

Jewish tradition expanded upon Judah's confession in Genesis 38.26, and further exonerated Tamar from any blame. Rahab was from the start a heroine in Jewish eyes, and she remained so: twice in the New Testament, in Hebrews and in the Letter of James, she is praised for the hospitality she showed the Israelite spies (Hebrews 11.31; James 2.25). Ruth's case is interesting. The ancient translations of her story and the rabbis who pass comment on it are keen to stress that she and Boaz did not have sex on the threshing floor. In fact, they probably read the story aright, since its subsequent passages make much easier sense if we believe they did not. Yet the mischievous ambiguities of the text of chapter 3 remain plain for all to see. As for Bathsheba, she tends to get hidden behind the substantial figure of her son, Solomon, or else caught up in the adulation surrounding David, but there were those who regarded her as an adulteress. After all, she was another man's wife when David had sex with her (Matthew himself points that out, of course), and many in the ancient world, and not just the Jewish one, would have assumed she seduced him and was as much to blame, if not more so, for what took place.

So what clues does Matthew leave us with as to why he includes these four in the list of Jesus' forebears? Not many, and none that are crystal clear, is the short answer. He does not explain himself, nor twist our arms to lead us screaming to a particular interpretation. And yet, as we have already remarked, when he comes in the next passage to speak of Mary's becoming pregnant with Jesus, he focuses on its disgrace, at least on the sense of shame and disgrace that takes hold of Joseph, until he learns from the angel that the Spirit of God is at work, that all is according to the ancient plans of God, that all is safe. The child to be born of Mary, he is told, is not to be despised. Rather, he should be hailed with cries of 'Emmanuel! God is with us!' And Mary is not to be scorned, either, but to be taken gladly as his wife.

Is this the clue? Surely Matthew means us to compare Mary with those four other women, with Tamar, Rahab, Ruth and 'the wife of Uriah', and conclude she was somehow like them. All four are on the edge; all four go, or are taken beyond where it is safe or deemed respectable for women to be; all four engage in sex that is outside the boundaries laid down, or come perilously close to doing so; all four find themselves at great risk. Is Matthew focusing on those things? If he is, then surely he means us also to recall that all four do the work of God as a result, and that in each case great good comes out of their actions.

Tamar plays the prostitute and risks not just her reputation, but her life; and yet out of that comes the saving of the family honour (as the men of her times would have conceived it), the lives of her twins, a future for Judah's name and family and, in due course, the coming into being of the tribe that bears his name.

For Rahab, prostitution is a way of life, and she is located on the very edge of Jericho as a result and, one would have thought, in the most vulnerable place in the event of an attack. And yet she uses, or rather, God uses both her trade and her place in Jericho to advance the cause of his people and bring them safely into the land promised for them. (Whatever our own feelings about the massacre at Jericho, that, no doubt, is how Matthew would wish us to interpret Rahab's story.)

The risk Ruth takes at the threshing floor is enormous. If it goes wrong, she will be branded a whore, not just by Boaz, but by the rest of the people of Bethlehem, and then where will she go? She is a foreigner, from Moab, as her story keeps reminding us. Already an outsider, she will be driven out of the village, if Boaz takes offence. But he does not, and all is well, and Ruth and Naomi are saved, and Naomi has a child to cuddle in the end and David a grandmother. 'Such are the mysterious ways of God,' I hear Matthew saying.

We do not know his opinion of Bathsheba, and whether or not he sees her as the victim of rape, but he can surely imagine the risk she takes when she announces her pregnancy to the king, and he knows also that her union with David leads eventually to the birth of Solomon, the 'wisest' of Israel's kings.

These women in Matthew's list both unnerve us and give us hope. Their inclusion hints that danger lurks and what might be regarded as sexual impropriety, and that Mary is going to find herself at great risk. At the same time it suggests that God is about to do a new thing and once more bring safety out of peril, honour out of dishonour, grace out of disgrace, good out of evil.

Matthew's list of names is not just a list of names.

# 4

## *Threatening disgrace*

———◆◆◆———

We step now from genealogy into storytelling. No one reads Matthew's list of names at Christmas carol services, but they do read the stories we are about to step into.

I choose my words carefully, when I speak of 'stepping into' the stories. Stories are not elaborations of doctrine – peel away their layers, and you get to the important bit. That is not their nature. The makers of doctrine strive for precision and clarity, for 'right' thinking. They set boundaries by which to define their community. Those who accept the doctrine are inside the community, those who do not are outside. That is how it has been; that is how it often is. In the history of the Christian Church those boundaries have sometimes had notices fixed to the inside of them (I speak metaphorically, you understand), saying in large letters, 'Thus far you may think, but no farther.' Formulated exclusively by powerful and clever men, doctrines have been used by them, or by other men in positions of leadership in the Church, to maintain or increase their authority, sometimes at the grievous expense of others. Storytellers, by contrast, seek for mystery. The finest storytellers of the Bible, including Matthew and Luke, delight in hints, allusion, ambiguity, meaning laid on meaning, and truth that is both captured and on the run. We do not step into the stories of Jesus' birth in either Matthew or Luke to be informed, to find out what we should believe. We go there to be moved, to find meaning and purpose, to find our place and a deeper understanding of ourselves and our world, to find hope, to find *God*, and to be changed. The producers of nativity plays, the painters, the poets, the film-makers know that, or some of it at least.

Knowing that ourselves, let us enter the first of Matthew's stories surrounding the birth of Jesus. 'Now the birth of Jesus the Messiah was like this. When his mother Mary had been betrothed to Joseph, but before they came together, she was found to be pregnant...' (1.18). That is not an auspicious start for one who is the Messiah!

Marriages in Jewish society in Jesus' day were in two parts, separated by up to a year. They were arranged by families, or rather by the men of those families, by the fathers. First came the betrothal, normally undertaken when the girl was coming up to puberty, or else had just arrived there. So we have to imagine a Mary much younger than the figure we are familiar with from paintings or statues, but not so very much older than the children who play her part in nativity plays, a Mary who is in her early or mid-teens, perhaps as young as 12. Betrothal meant much more than being engaged in our own society (which is why it is better to avoid the term 'engaged' in our translation of Matthew's text). It involved a formal exchange in the presence of witnesses of an agreement to marry. From that moment the girl counted as the man's wife, and he as her husband. Yet though he had certain legal rights over her, she remained living with her parents, still to a large extent under her father's authority. If her husband had due cause, he could divorce her. If she was charged with having sex with another man, she could be accused of adultery. If the man died before the marriage was completed, she counted as his widow. At the end of about a year the second part of the marriage was conducted, when the girl would be taken from her parents' house to that of her husband. From then on they would live together, and she would be under his authority and his protection. Whether they were allowed to have sexual relations during the period of the betrothal became a moot point in Judaism, with some claiming it was permissible, and others insisting that sexual intercourse was part of the completion of the marriage. It may be that debate did not arise till some decades after Jesus was born. In any case, as we shall see, the inhabitants of Matthew's Bethlehem appear to take the stricter line. All this has to be understood before we can enter the world of Matthew's story of Jesus, before we can catch the suspense that is there, the fear, the darkness of the looming disgrace.

The story continues with this: 'Her husband Joseph, being a righteous man and not wishing to expose her to public disgrace, planned to divorce her quietly' (1.19). We have left out a crucial phrase from the end of the previous verse. That concludes, Mary 'was found to be pregnant from the Holy Spirit'. However we understand that phrase, and we will come to that in due course, it clearly makes all the difference. But Joseph does not know that yet. For him Mary's pregnancy seems a catastrophe.

But notice it is *his* problem, not Mary's. That is how Matthew has written the story. Though Joseph will be strangely absent from the story of the visit of the magi in the next chapter, and despite the fact that Matthew never gives him anything to say (the angel does all the talking), he generally plays a much more prominent role than Mary in these stories of Jesus' birth. When we come to Luke's stories, we will discover the roles are reversed, with Mary taking centre stage. Matthew has already given us Joseph's genealogy. Despite his not being Jesus' biological father, the long list of names gives us his ancestry, not Mary's. Joseph will be mentioned by name seven times (Mary only four times); he will receive four messages in dreams from an angel; the fate of Mary and her child is in his hands and will depend always on his obedience, not hers. Heaven speaks to Joseph, but not to Mary; his righteousness is tested, not hers; his understanding is needed, while she will simply go along with what he decides. What Mary thinks, what Mary believes is immaterial, and what Mary decides . . . well, Mary is never in a position to decide, or take any initiative.

To us that can seem most shocking. To many of us it *is* shocking. Yet we must realize Matthew is reflecting the attitudes and assumptions of his day, and the usual conventions of his Scriptures, too. That is not to condone the line he takes, but it is to understand it better. We have seen already from our explanation of marriage and betrothal that the procedures were devised entirely for the benefit of the man and to a lesser degree the fathers of the families involved. They assumed the husband had authority over his wife, and were designed to establish and maintain his power. The attitudes they enshrined are not, of course, absent from our own contemporary world, but indeed sometimes find such terrible expression as would have shocked the good people of Matthew's Bethlehem, including the men. For countless women today things are worse than they were in Jesus' day. Yet, as the story proceeds, let us pay heed to Mary's powerlessness.

Joseph is faced with a dilemma. He seems to face it on his own, till heaven intervenes. He does not meet with Mary or, if he does, we do not hear of it. He does not discuss it with Jacob his father, not on the page of the story, nor is there any discussion between Jacob and Mary's father. Who knows about this pregnancy? A superb Channel 4 television programme a few Christmases ago, which tried on the basis of the work of historians and archaeologists to give us a portrait of the historical Mary hidden behind the figure of Christian devotion, in one dramatized scene showed Mary hiding behind her mother's skirts as her mother broke the news of the pregnancy to her father. It was a telling moment. But that scene does not appear in Matthew. His writing is sparse, leaving much to our imaginations, inviting us to fill its silences. He leaves us with the loneliness, the isolation of Joseph. We have to work against the grain of his text to imagine Mary's.

Joseph is not faced with the question of whether or not to divorce Mary. She is pregnant, and he knows the child is not his, because they have not yet had any sexual relations with one another. He has no choice. By all the thinking of his times he must divorce her. The question is whether or not he should keep the matter between the two families, or whether he should bring the matter into the open. Should Mary be questioned in public and an attempt be made to discover who the father is, and whether she was raped, or consented? If we were at Joseph's side, we might remind him how young Mary is, and that she does not live in a society where girls of her age are given freedom to hang around on the streets and do their own thing. But Joseph lives in a world where it could be said, 'The wife of an Israelite who has been outraged [that is raped] is forbidden to her husband, *since it may be apprehended that the act begun under compulsion may have terminated with her consent.*' (My italics; the rabbinic saying is quoted by Jane

Schaberg in her book, *The Illegitimacy of Jesus*, 1995, p. 48).
Back in 2004 I remember reading a story in the newspaper of
two Iraqi sisters who had been kidnapped and sold into prostitution in the Yemen. One was already married. The story of
their escape was a long, complex and harrowing one, but eventually they made it back to their own country. Yet only the
unmarried one had returned home. The husband of the other
sister was demanding a divorce, and when she refused, her
own brother threatened to kill her, 'because she had brought
such disgrace upon the family'. *She* had brought them disgrace! She and her sister had been through hell, but in her
husband's eyes she was dirty, soiled goods and that was that,
while her brother was so sure of her husband's authority, and
of what constituted his family's precious honour, that he lost
sight of her humanity altogether.

Thank God, Joseph is not like that woman's brother! Yet
he belongs to a similar culture, where the honour of men is
paramount, and where women are sacrificed so that it can be
restored or maintained. He decides to divorce Mary 'quietly',
keeping the matter between the two families. What will she
say once her child is born and all the village knows? He will
leave her and her parents to sort that one out.

But then comes the turning point:

> But just when he had resolved to do this, behold an angel
> of the Lord appeared to him in a dream, saying, 'Joseph,
> son of David, do not be afraid to take Mary as your wife,
> for the child conceived in her is from the Holy Spirit. She
> will bear a son, and you shall give him his name, Jesus.
> For he will save his people from their sins.'   (1.20–21)

Matthew's Gospel begins and ends with an angel. Here in these
birth stories the angel determines the course of events, and it
will reappear to announce the resurrection of Jesus to Mary
of Magdala and Mary the mother of James and Joseph. There
also its first words will be: 'Do not be afraid.'

And we hardly notice the change of gear! For Matthew
writes as if there has not been any, except, perhaps, for his
insertion of that small word, 'behold', even shorter in the
Greek and so seemingly insignificant, that modern translations

often leave it out. Yet suddenly, with the dreaming Joseph, we find ourselves taken out of this world and into heaven, transported across the shining line that divides the earthly from the divine. And heaven talks and both we and Joseph can understand it! Or we *think* we can.

Yet why does it need an angel? Why does not God himself speak with Joseph? If this story were in Genesis, he would, or rather talk of 'an angel' would be no more than a pious circumlocution, a way of speaking of the very presence of God. But then Genesis presents us with a garden where God makes and moulds with his hands, where he walks in the cool of the day, and with a God who wrestles with a man through the hours of darkness and begs to be released. In the famous story of Jacob's ladder in Genesis 28, God himself comes down to stand beside the sleeping Jacob, to speak of promise and re-assurance, to declare, 'Know that I am with you and will keep you wherever you go' (28.15a). Yet such a bold way of speaking is highly unusual in the Bible. Beyond the Moses stories in Exodus God retreats into transcendence, as someone has put it, and we are left for the most part with a God who is presented to us as more distant, more set apart in his own world. Soon in Matthew's Gospel this God will split the heavens apart and speak – at Jesus' baptism in 3.16–17 – and at the moment of Jesus' death the curtain of the Jerusalem temple, the one that keeps God hidden from sight in the Holy of Holies, will be torn from top to bottom (27.51) and God will roam free. But for now an angel must suffice, and we must be content with such a veiled reference to the bright intimacy of God.

We might have expected the angel to appear to Mary, not Joseph, and not just because the angel Gabriel does in Luke's parallel story. For this is what we call 'an annunciation story', and there are others in the Old Testament which will have been somewhere in Matthew's mind as he wrote, two of which put the mother centre stage.

In Genesis 16, God appears to the Egyptian Hagar to tell her,

Now you have conceived and shall bear a son;
you shall call him Ishmael,
for the Lord has given heed to your affliction.

29

> He shall be a wild ass of a man,
> with his hand against everyone,
> and everyone's hand against him;
> and he shall live at odds with all his kin.
> (Genesis 16.11–12)

In the very next chapter of Genesis God speaks to Abraham: 'Your wife Sarah shall bear you a son, and you shall name him Isaac. I will establish my covenant with him as an everlasting covenant for his offspring after him' (17.19). In the story following that, God appears to Abraham in the heat of the day, when Sarah is inside the tent. She is close enough to hear the words addressed to her husband, 'I will surely return to you at life-tide, and your wife Sarah shall have a son' (18.10, 'lifetide' is Mary Korsak's brilliant translation in *At the start . . . Genesis made new*, 1992, p. 58). Finally, Judges 13 contains the somewhat mischievous story of an appearance of God to 'the wife of Manoah', or Eluma as the rabbis came to call her, when she too is promised a child: 'Although you are barren, having borne no children, you shall conceive and bear a son . . . It is he who shall begin to deliver Israel from the hand of the Philistines' (Judges 13.3b, 5b).

Mary 'will bear a son, and you shall give him his name, Jesus. For he will save his people from their sins' (Matthew 1.21). Matthew is clearly keeping to the established pattern here, one that leads him back to the very origins of his people, when the promises of God crackle in the air for the first time.

The annunciation stories in the Bible bring the divine very close, and into the midst of risk and despair. When God appears to Hagar in Genesis 16, she is a runaway slave in the desert. Her mistress Sarah has so abused her she cannot take it any more and has escaped, carrying Abraham's child with her in her womb. The story is double-edged, since the God who meets her sends her back to her mistress, and yet his declaration about her child turns her from a runaway slave into the ancestress of a great people, and promises her that the day will come when she will be free, at nobody's beck and call, beyond the reach of the curse and the striking hand. As for Sarah, by the time Genesis 17 and 18 arrive, the years of waiting for a child have turned to decades, and the hope of ever having one has long gone for both her and Abraham. Yet now she will have a son, who with a name like Isaac will come straight from the laughter of God (Isaac means in the Hebrew 'he laughs'), and will carry forward the bright promises of God and the command, first issued to Abraham in Genesis 12.2, to be a blessing to all the families of the earth. Eluma, the wife of Manoah, lives in lawless and highly dangerous times, when the Israelite tribes are suffering grievously at the hands of their neighbours, the Philistines. Her son will bring those tribes some respite and some power. And she herself has been years without children, in a world where women are chiefly valued for the children and especially the sons they produce for their husbands.

Each of these annunciations stories is unique, yet they all speak of hopes and expectations raised far beyond what has been thought possible, of the finding of a new dignity and the establishment of a new status for those who have little or none of either, of 'disgrace' being turned through grace to grace.

That is true not only for Hagar, Sarah and Eluma, but for Joseph and Mary, also. Before the angel speaks Joseph thinks he has no choice but to divorce Mary. Before the angel speaks her pregnancy threatens to ruin everything, and all Joseph can do is to try to limit the shame and the disgrace of it. Our imaginations tell us he will probably not succeed: the pain and anger of their families will spill out into the streets of the village; Mary's father and brothers will be scorned because they did not control her and protect her virginity; Joseph will be the butt of cruel jokes: 'Couldn't look after your woman, then, Joseph!'; Mary will be called 'a whore' and her child, once it is born, will be 'a bastard' for the rest of its life. After the angel has spoken Joseph realizes there is another option open to him, the most humane and compassionate one, to go ahead and complete the marriage and take Mary home to live with him. Everyone will surely assume the child she carries is his, and though they might tut-tut a bit, the shame he and Mary will have to endure will be short-lived and nothing to compare with that of a divorce.

So that is indeed what Joseph does: 'When Joseph awoke from sleep, he did as the angel of the Lord commanded him; he took her as his wife, but had no sexual relations with her until she gave birth to a son; and he called his name Jesus' (Matthew 1.24).

What makes all the difference, however, is not just the angel's appearing, but its telling Joseph that the child in Mary's womb is 'from the Holy Spirit'. We, the readers or hearers of the story, were let into the secret near the beginning. So what does that phrase mean? It is time to address that question.

For many, Matthew himself supplies the answer. Near the end of the passage he inserts a comment of his own that is plainly meant to help us understand what is going on:

All this took place to fulfil what had been spoken by the Lord through the prophet:

'Behold, the virgin shall conceive and bear a son,
and they shall call his name Emmanuel',

which means, 'God with us.'                    (1.22–23)

If we bring this quotation of Isaiah 7.14 to bear on the twice repeated phrase 'from the Holy Spirit', then the meaning might seem to be clear: Matthew is speaking of a virgin birth, of a Mary who has not had sexual relations with anyone at all, of a child conceived through a creative act of God, a child, we might say, direct from God. Many within scholarship believe that is indeed what Matthew is saying. In the final chapter of this book we will discuss the doctrine of the virgin birth and give our own assessment of it. For the time being we are simply interested in teasing out what Matthew means us to hear.

In truth there is a greater degree of ambiguity in his story than is often acknowledged. It makes little difference whether we say, 'Behold, the virgin shall conceive', or, 'Behold, the young woman shall conceive.' The Hebrew of Isaiah 7.14 has the word *alma*, which translates as 'young woman', and might or might not refer to a virgin. Matthew quotes the ancient Greek translation of the Old Testament, known as the Septuagint, from where he gets the Greek term *parthenos* which usually does mean virgin, but need not do so – in translating Genesis 34.3 the authors call an unmarried woman named Dinah a *parthenos*, although she has been raped. Almost certainly in Isaiah 7.14 they are using *parthenos* in its usual sense, but they do not imagine Isaiah is talking of a virgin birth in the sense we mean. No doubt they assume he is predicting that a young woman, at the time a virgin, will soon conceive through perfectly natural means and bear a son.

Who Isaiah's young woman or virgin was remains a mystery. She may have been a girl Isaiah himself was about to marry. The passage concerned presents us with the prophet trying to reassure King Ahaz in Jerusalem at a time of great crisis, when the Syrians and those from the northern kingdom of Israel are threatening to attack the city. 'The heart of Ahaz and the heart of his people shook as the trees of the forest shake before the wind,' we are told (Isaiah 7.2b). Isaiah tells the king to stand firm in faith, to be calm, to lose his fear. 'All will be well,' he says (I paraphrase). 'A child will be born to a girl, a firstborn son, and he will be a living sign of God's presence and protection, for his name will be "God with us!".' The significance of the child for Isaiah and Ahaz, however we translate the Hebrew or the Greek of verse 14, will lie not in any unusual means of conception, but in the timing of his birth and the character of his name.

Returning to Matthew, we now find everything hangs on those words 'from (in the Greek, *ek*) the Holy Spirit'. And he does not explain them! In his list of names, when he speaks of the children of Tamar, Rahab, Ruth or Bathsheba, he describes them as being born 'from' (*ek*) these women. Does he imply that the Holy Spirit is in some sense 'the parent' of Jesus, not the mother in his case, of course, but the father? It would seem he does. Yet that does not necessarily imply that he is speaking of a virgin birth, nor that he is ruling out a human father. In his Letter to the Galatians, Paul describes the people of God as having been 'born according to the Spirit' (Galatians 4.29), while in his Gospel, John has Jesus talk to the Pharisee Nicodemus about being 'born of (*ek*) the Spirit' (John 3.5, 6, 8). In the Prologue he distinguishes between those born of flesh and blood and those born of God: 'But to all those who received him, who believed in his name, he gave power to become children of God, who were born not of (*ek*) blood or of (*ek*) the will of the flesh or of (*ek*) the will of man, but of (*ek*) God' (John 1.12–13). This is clearly figurative language, and John goes out of his way to make sure we do not take it literally. Nicodemus, in his dialogues with Jesus, does just that, and starts asking how someone can re-enter their mother's womb once they have grown up. Jesus explains that he is not talking in such literal terms. Why then should we approach Matthew any differently?

If Matthew is talking figuratively, then we can hear the angel saying something like this to Joseph: 'Do not be afraid! Mary's pregnancy is not the catastrophe you suppose. For the Spirit of God is at work here, and has wrapped itself round the child in her womb, turning the ugliness and violence of rape into something of lasting hope and beauty. Far from being mired in another's sin, Mary is carrying the very forgiveness of God within her womb, a child who will embody God's saving power. You think you are faced with a tragedy so small in world terms that no one outside Bethlehem will ever hear of it, but one so large for you, Mary and your two families, that you will all be consumed by it. You are wrong in every way, my friend! Mary is carrying the world's salvation, a salvation for all, which nothing will ever be able to defeat! Do the humane, the compassionate thing, Joseph. Complete the marriage, take Mary to your home, adopt the child, and then he can have your pedigree, Joseph, son of David. He needs your cooperation if he is to be called Messiah, which in truth he is, for his descent must be traced through you. Do not be afraid, Joseph, join in the work of God, for you are in the midst of a miracle greater than you can comprehend. You are within touching distance of the immensity of God!'

Oh, the marvellous, liberating ambiguity of biblical storytelling, where whole worlds can be held in the palm of a few words!

And who then is the father of Mary's child? If we understand the angel in the second way I have suggested, then we do not know. A man in the village, no doubt. A man without a name, who hides in the dark shadows of the story and never emerges into the sun where we can see him. A man whose sordid, demeaning act has been turned by God into the greatest possible good. A man who in more ways than one does not begin to know what he has done.

# 5

## *Two kings and some magi*

This is a story of two kings, not three. It begins like this:

> When Jesus was born in Bethlehem of Judea in the days
> of Herod the king, behold magi from the east arrived in
> Jerusalem, asking, 'Where is the newborn king of the
> Jews? For we saw his star in the east and have come to
> worship him.' When Herod the king heard this, he was
> scared out of his wits and all Jerusalem with him.
> Gathering together all the chief priests and scribes of the
> people, he enquired of them where the Christ was to be
> born. 'In Bethlehem of Judea,' they told him. 'For thus it
> is written by the prophet:
>
>> "And you, Bethlehem, in the land of Judah,
>> are by no means least among the rulers of Judah;
>> for from you shall come a ruler
>> who will shepherd my people Israel."
>
> Then Herod secretly called for the magi, to learn from
> them the exact time of the star's appearance.'    (2.1–7)

Both Matthew and Luke place Jesus' birth in Bethlehem, a village a few miles from Jerusalem. It was famous in the tradition as the setting for the story of Ruth and Naomi, and even
more, of course, as the home village of David. By the time
Jesus was born, David had been dead for over 950 years, yet
still he was celebrated as the greatest king the Jews had ever
had and, what is more, he was one of their own. Herod was
from Idumea, and although his father counted himself as a
Jew and was regarded as such by his contemporaries, he had
no royal pedigree. He was 'king of the Jews' in Jerusalem because the Roman government had befriended him and given
him the title. His kingdom belonged to the Roman Empire.

In this political context, Bethlehem is not the insignificant place it might seem, not in Matthew's story, at least. Whether it was actually the case that the Jewish religious leaders of the day expected the Messiah to come from Bethlehem is unclear. John 7 presents us with two opposing views: some in Jerusalem claim that 'when the Messiah comes, no one will know where he is from' (7.27); others say, 'Has not the scripture said that the Messiah is descended from David and comes from Bethlehem, the village where David lived?' (7.42). In Matthew's story of the magi, the religious hierarchy are in no doubt at all. Without any hesitation they mark Bethlehem as the place, and quote Micah 5.2 and 2 Samuel 5.2 to prove it. In fact, they misquote Micah and turn one of his lines on its head. For Micah reads in the Hebrew:

> But you, O Bethlehem of Ephrathah,
> small though you are among the clans of Judah,
> from you shall come forth for me
> one who is to rule in Israel,

and in the Greek Septuagint the 'small' of the second line is strengthened to 'smallest' or 'least significant'. But their mistake matters not. Out of their Scriptures they have picked out Micah 5 and Bethlehem. As far as Matthew is concerned, they are spot on, particularly if they recall another verse in Micah 5 that soon follows the one quoted.

> And he shall stand and feed his flock in the strength of
>     the LORD,
> in the majesty of the name of the LORD his God.
> And they shall live secure, for now he shall be great
> to the ends of the earth;
> and he shall be the one of peace.
>
> (Micah 5.4)

No wonder Herod is scared out of his wits. *He* is the king of the Jews. Now there are magi roaming around Jerusalem asking about another 'king of the Jews' and saying he has just been born, and his religious leaders calmly tell him the birthplace is just six miles away, in David's own village. What is more, the magi have seen his star!

But who are these 'magi'? Christian tradition has done a lot of work on them. It has turned them into kings, given them kingdoms, nationalities, different colours of skin, and names. They have become Balthasar, the king of Chaldea, usually portrayed in Christian art as a white man; Gaspar, the Ethiopian king of Tarshish, pictured as a brown man; and Melchior, the black king of Nubia. In doing that to them writers and artists have added a further dimension to Matthew's story, and many of the images in Western art of kings dressed in rich and elaborate costumes kneeling before a small baby, who lies in the arms of his mother in the ruin of a stable, have a particular poignancy about them. And yet, at the same time they have blunted the sharpness of Matthew's tale.

There is no doubt his magi are rich. The gifts they present to the child Jesus later in the story are extremely expensive. But they are not kings. Nor are they 'wise men', though some of our most respected English versions would have it so. The *New English Bible* and the *Revised English Bible* translate Matthew's Greek word *magoi* as 'astrologers' and, if we must translate the word at all, that is probably the best option. Better still, leave it as it is and just transliterate it. Let it remain 'magi', with the strangeness, the sense of mystery and the ambiguities that term conveys.

For magi get a decidedly mixed press in the literature of the ancient world. They came originally from Persia, beyond the eastern boundaries of the Roman Empire. The Roman poet Juvenal, writing soon after Matthew's time, derides people from the east as among the low life of the city, mixed up with drink and prostitutes, full of superstition and naïve belief in astrology. Before him the Roman intelligentsia speak more specifically of 'the nonsense' put about by magi, their 'fraudulent lies', their ridiculous predictions. Philo, also, a highly educated Jew who lived in Alexandria at the time of Jesus, tells of innocent and gullible people being duped by the magi and their enchantments. The word *magoi* appears once in the Septuagint, in Daniel 2, where they appear in the court of King Nebuchadnezzar with his magicians and sorcerers and other 'experts', and are quite unable to rise to the admittedly stiff challenge of telling the king the details of a dream he has had and then interpreting it. The hero of that story, Daniel the Jew, is given both dream and interpretation in a 'vision of the night'.

Yet notice how the book of Daniel has magi walking the corridors of power. There we catch sight of the other side of their story. Many believed they could indeed interpret the movement of stars and could thereby predict the fall of kings or empires, or the births of new rulers. Kings might well consult them, and sometimes did, and they could genuinely fear what they had to tell them.

We find these conflicting views of magi either on the surface of Matthew's story, or else concealed just beneath its surface. What are they doing blundering about Jerusalem, asking questions about a new 'king of the Jews'? As some have said, not a particularly wise thing to do! It is one matter to storm into the palace of the incumbent monarch, and face him with claims that his time is up. It is quite another to go round the streets questioning the general populace, when Herod's magnificent palace, and his even more magnificent temple stare them in the face and blind their eyes with their splendour. Does it not occur to them to make enquiries first about who is in power? Seemingly not. And, of course, their precious star has brought them to the wrong place. Looking for a king, and loaded with presents they think fit, they assume he must be found in what is clearly the centre of power in that part of the world. Not only are they in the wrong place, but they are looking for quite the wrong kind of king.

Yet their claims cause general alarm and are taken very seriously indeed by Herod. When he learns of the word on the street, he at once summons his top religious advisors, and then the magi themselves. He does not dispute the magi's ability to read the stars. He only needs to learn their precise evidence. On the basis of that he accepts without any further question their larger claim that a new 'king' is born. His own experts are needed merely to fill in the detail of the birthplace.

Matthew's own attitude towards the magi is ambivalent. The first ones to recognize the significance of Jesus' birth beyond Joseph (Mary is so hidden in the shadows of his narrative, that we do not know what she herself thinks!), the first ones to come and worship him, they are outsiders in more ways than one. They are not Jews; they have come from 'the east', where, so people say, too much superstitious nonsense comes from; they are magi, too often charged with perpetrating that same nonsense. And on the streets of Jerusalem they seem to be especially naïve and foolish. Yet they have caught the movement of the star. No one else has seen it, but they have, and they have realized, too, what it means, the birth of a new king, the birth of a king of the Jews. And though they have expected to find him in the Jerusalems of this world, rather than in a Bethlehem, and so have allowed themselves to be misled, nevertheless they have travelled hundreds of miles to come within a stone's throw of the place where Jesus lies. They certainly have their cleverness, even their wisdom. Indeed, they are wiser than they know, for unwittingly they have embarked upon the most significant journey of all, and at its end will find not just a king (the strangest king in all the world!), but a God.

And what are *we* to make of them, and especially of their star? Recent Christmases have seen endless and predictable discussions in newspapers or on radio about which star it might have been, and solemn argument has been maintained about this or that constellation, conjunction of planets, comet or supernova. Such discussions do more harm than good. They are fruitless, for they are based on the false assumption that Matthew is a reporter of events, rather than a creative artist; they miss the star's deeper significance; and they must in the minds of many engender a needless scepticism, and a rejection of Matthew's story, and with it his whole Gospel (if not the entire Bible!) as patently ridiculous and 'untrue'. 'For God's sake', they might say, 'this star moves against the general swing of the heavens, leads the magi down a particular road and then stops not just above a particular village, but a particular house! It is impossible, the stuff of children's stories and nativity plays, but not for the mature, rational mind: for the gullible believer, perhaps, but not for the person who thinks!'

Let us not pretend. Of course this star is impossible. That is the whole point. It is a storyteller's star, and good storytellers are skilled at suspending our disbelief. Matthew is an extremely good storyteller, and if only we will take his star with the right kind of seriousness, we will have no problems with it. Rather, we will take great delight in it, derive comfort from it, be profoundly, but properly, unnerved by it.

First, let us recall how small this star is. In some paintings of the magi and on many Christmas cards of the scene we see a whacking great blob of light that dominates the night sky and could only be missed by someone who was completely blind. It is very nice of the painters and the card designers to give Jesus such a big star, but he does not need it, and they do Matthew, the word artist, a disservice. For Matthew's star is tiny to the eye, as all stars are, and its rising and movement across the sky so inconspicuous that only the magi, with their trained eyes fixed upon the heavens, see it. No one else does. Only they pick out its tiny point of light among the myriads of others and catch its movement, its strange exactitude.

The magi and their author belong to a time when people spoke of a star brightening when someone was born and dimming when they died, and there were stories around of strange heavenly phenomena being associated with the births of such as Augustus, Tiberius or Nero, emperors of Rome. The great Roman poet Virgil, writing in the century before Christ, speaks of a star guiding Aeneas, the founder of Rome, to the spot where the city should be built. When we consider Matthew's story of the magi, we must be careful not to dismiss such stories as empty tales for, like his, they are heavy with meaning. For they claim that the birth (or death) of a person is so significant an event that the very pattern of the heavens is changed, and that occasionally the change is so marked that we can tell the person is of truly momentous importance.

We may not belong to such a time, though echoes of its beliefs still clearly sound. We can, however, catch and hold in our hands the meaning of Matthew's strange star. But we have to use metaphor to describe that meaning, and only poetic speech will do. And so we say that the star leads the magi and us to a child whose crying resounds throughout the universe, to a God who plays sliding down the curling banisters of the

41

galaxies, to a God whose embrace reaches the furthest star and far beyond (for has not Matthew already told us this small child is Emmanuel, God with us?). Matthew's star will prevent us from making his story too parochial, and its God too small. It will remind us that Jesus' birth is an event of truly cosmic significance.

And it will help us be properly astonished by the place of the child's birth. Let us return to the text of the story.

Then Herod secretly called for the magi, to learn from them the exact time of the star's appearance. Then he sent them to Bethlehem saying, 'Go and find out exactly where the child is, and when you have found him, bring me word, that I also may go and worship him.' When they had heard the king, they set out, and behold, the star which they saw in the east went before them, until it came and stopped above where the child was. Seeing the star, they rejoiced with exceeding great joy, and going into the house they saw the child with Mary his mother, and falling on their knees they worshipped him. Then they opened their treasures, and presented him with gifts, gold, frankincense, and myrrh. And being warned of God in a dream not to return to Herod, they left for their own country by a different road.

When they had left, behold, an angel of the Lord appeared to Joseph in a dream saying, 'Get up, take the child and his mother and flee to Egypt and remain there until I tell you. For Herod is about to search for the child, to destroy him.' So Joseph got up, took the child and his mother in the middle of the night, and left for Egypt, and remained there until the death of Herod. This was to fulfil what was spoken by the Lord through the prophet, saying, 'Out of Egypt I have called my son.'

Then Herod, realizing the magi had made a fool of him, became extremely angry and sent and killed all the children in Bethlehem and in that entire region who were two years old and under, according to the time he had learned from the magi. Then was fulfilled what was spoken through the prophet Jeremiah, saying,

'A voice was heard in Ramah,
wailing and loud lamentation:
Rachel weeping for her children;
she refused to be consoled, because they are no more.'

(2.7–18)

We hear of two kings here, and two kinds of sovereignty. On the one hand, we have Herod in his grand palace, in his capital city, used to summoning people to his presence and having them come running, who finds it easy to lie when he has to (see how he tells the magi of his intention of going to Bethlehem to 'worship' the child), who has troops to hand who will obey any order he gives. He has huge power, or so he thinks, but he is terrified he might lose it. He has great honour to preserve, also, and cannot bear being made to look a fool. He is given to rages and to paranoia, and believes his honour must be recovered, his power maintained at all costs. If it takes the deaths of a few dozen infants and babies, so be it.

On the other side, we have the newborn King Jesus and the decidedly strange sovereignty of God. We have a God who is 'with us', lying seemingly helpless in an insignificant house in an insignificant village. The magi fall to their knees and worship. They find they can do no other. Earlier, in Herod's palace, they did not prostrate themselves, but with the small child and his mother they find themselves at once on holy ground.

They offer what they have brought, expensive gifts such as the Herods of their world would expect or demand. In the small family house in Bethlehem, those must seem strangely out of place, except that Matthew's Scriptures have led us to think them appropriate. There is a justly famous passage in Isaiah, which pictures the restoration of Jerusalem after the trauma of the Babylonian exile, and which is often read in Christmas carol services. 'Arise, shine; for your light has come, and the glory of the LORD has risen upon you,' it begins (Isaiah 60.1), and it continues with:

Nations shall come to your light,
and kings to the brightness of your dawn.

(60.3)

A multitude of camels shall cover you,
the young camels of Midian and Ephah;
all those from Sheba shall come.
They shall bring gold and frankincense,
and shall proclaim the praise of the LORD.
(60.6)

Other passages tell of the richness of myrrh and sometimes
associate it with frankincense. Psalm 45 was originally composed for a royal wedding, and showers the king with extravagant praise, comparing him even to a god:

Your throne, O God, endures for ever and ever.
Your royal sceptre is a sceptre of equity;
you love righteousness and hate wickedness.
Therefore God, your God, has anointed you
with the oil of gladness beyond your companions;
your robes are all fragrant with myrrh and aloes and
cassia.

(Ps. 45.6–8a)

The young woman of the passionate love poems of the Song
of Songs sings these lines of the man she loves, and compares
him to king Solomon:

Who is that rising from the desert
like a pillar of smoke,
more fragrant with myrrh and frankincense,
than all the spices of the merchant!
Oh the splendours of King Solomon!
. . . Come out, O daughters of Zion,
and gaze at Solomon the King!
(Song of Songs 3.6–7a, 11a, Chana and
Ariel Bloch's 1998 translation)

In a later poem the man replies:

An enclosed garden is my sister, my bride,
a hidden well, a sealed spring.
Your branches are an orchard
Of pomegranate trees heavy with fruit,
flowering henna and spikenard,

spikenard and saffron, cane and cinnamon,
with every tree of frankincense,
myrrh and aloes,
all the rare spices.

(4.12–14, again Chana and
Ariel Bloch's and translation)

The verses from Isaiah, together with others from the Psalms
(see Psalm 72.10–11, 15), will have encouraged the later devel-
opment of Matthew's story, the turning of the magi into kings,
and even the inclusion of their camels. Together all these passages underline how luxurious the magi's gifts are, presents
truly fit for a king. Towards the end of the second century
the theologian Irenaeus suggested that gold, frankincense and
myrrh should be seen as symbols of Christ's kingship, priesthood and divinity, and passion and death. This interpretation
is still popular. It features in the Christmas carol, 'We three
kings of orient are,' and in many a Christmas or Epiphany
sermon. It is unlikely, however, that it was in Matthew's own
mind. Mark, in his story of Jesus' crucifixion, talks of him
being offered 'wine mixed with myrrh' (15.23). No doubt that
is why Irenaeus thinks of the myrrh given by the magi as a
symbol of the death Jesus is to suffer. Yet significantly, when
Matthew comes to Mark's text, he changes it to 'wine . . .
mixed with gall' (27.34); for him the fragrance of myrrh is
*not* present at Golgotha, but instead a wine that has been
mixed with something that is both bitter and poisonous.

The magi offering their gifts is the high point of Matthew's
whole story of the birth of Jesus. It is truly wonderful, and
the painters, the poets and the makers of carols do well to
make us pause and reflect. Matthew himself does not allow
us that luxury. He hurries on and takes us out into the pitch
dark. The magi themselves are not permitted to linger. No
sooner are their gifts handed over than they are warned by
God not to return to Herod. In that small house in Bethlehem
and in the child lying in the arms of that young girl, Mary,
they have found the kingdom of heaven and realized how very
different it is from the kingdom of Herod. They are wiser now.
With God opening their sleeping eyes, they can see through

Herod's fearful duplicity. They will not be instrumental in his coming to Bethlehem to 'worship' the small child. They can guess all too easily what he has in mind. They will not become his informers, and so they leave by another road and have nothing more to do with Jerusalem, or its terrified king.

They try to do what is for the best. They heed God's warning. They are obedient and neither question nor hesitate. And yet their failure to return to Herod sparks off terrible events, that remind us of some of the darkest places in the world. First Joseph must get up in the night, not to sing Jesus a lullaby after his feed, but to pick him up, wake the exhausted Mary, and hurry out into the darkness of the village streets, into the vast emptiness of the desert hills beyond, and on and on and on, never daring to look back. No longer is Jesus surrounded by gleaming, pungent gifts that make his home shine and smell like a palace. He is now a refugee, and being newborn and out of reach of the hands of Bethlehem women who are used to looking after babies, and with a very young mother who has scarcely begun to recover from the rigours of labour, he is in very great danger. Will he or Mary survive the journey? If we use our imaginations and fill some of the gaps Matthew leaves for us, we cannot help but ask the question, nor will we find it a casual one. Far too many women will know the dangers this Jesus and Mary face, and Joseph also, and will remember their own journeys, and the bodies of those who did not make it, lying huddled, too still, by the side of the road.

Joseph leads his wife and child for day upon day, until they reach the safety of Egypt. Thus they re-enact the ancient story of their people, the Jews, and call to our minds another Joseph, sold into slavery in Egypt by his brothers, then later giving them and their families, together with their father Jacob, sanctuary from famine of Canaan. Egypt's fertility is their salvation, and allows them over generations to be 'fruitful and prolific, to multiply and grow exceedingly strong' (see Exodus 1.7). For Jesus and his parents what matters is that Egypt is outside Herod's jurisdiction.

For the most part Matthew leaves it to us to make these connections with the stories of Genesis and Exodus, though,

to prompt us, he does briefly quote the prophet Hosea and
that exquisite poem of his which begins:

When Israel was a child, I loved him,
*and out of Egypt I called my son.*
(Hosea 11.1, my italics)

His quotations of the biblical text, and his veiled references
to it, such as we saw also in his description of the gifts of
the magi, serve a common purpose: to demonstrate that the
events surrounding the birth of Jesus fit into an ancient and
sacred pattern. They are not random; they have long been
predicted; they belong to the eternal plan of God, and to his
talent for bringing good out of evil. The more unexpected,
the more shocking they might seem, the more necessary it is
to show how they relate to Scripture and its sacred tales.

So even Herod's sending his soldiers to kill the babies and
small children in and around Bethlehem, and the mothers
they leave in the streets wailing their bitter grief and refusing
to be consoled, even that for Matthew has been foreseen by
Jeremiah, and the prophet's poetry comes to most terrible
fulfilment. Our own minds will turn not to Jeremiah, but the
stories we have heard coming out of Auschwitz, Rwanda,
Dafur or, with strange and fearful irony, from Lebanon, or
Gaza, or even Bethlehem itself, where too many children have
lost their lives through violence, or live in terror of soldiers
with their guns and tanks and bulldozers, and the sonic booms
of heavily armed fighter jets. It is not only the Jewish Rachel
who weeps in Ramah now.

In Matthew's story of the birth of Jesus, the magi are *the
only ones* who worship him as he deserves. When the magi
arrive in Jerusalem they set the whole city talking. That is how
Matthew tells it. They do not set the place alight with joy and
excitement, however, but shroud it in fear. Herod is scared out
of his wits by the magi's news that a new king has been born,
but so is 'all Jerusalem with him'. And when the magi go
on the final, short leg of their journey to Bethlehem, they
go alone. There is no carnival procession, as there should be.
They are not accompanied by the trumpet sound, tambourine,
dance and loud clashing cymbals of Psalm 150. The road

echoes to nothing but the sound of their feet and, once they have gone, will fall silent again, until Herod's soldiers stamp into it the march of his tyranny and fear.

As we wrote in our opening chapter, Matthew's fragile Jesus is a candle in a dark world, where the breeze of human frailty and the storm of men's concern for their power and honour threaten to blow out its flame, and so nearly, so nearly succeed.

# 6

## *No going home*

We have nearly reached the end of Matthew's stories of the birth of Jesus. There is just one more passage to consider, and it is short:

> When Herod died, behold, an angel of the Lord appeared to Joseph in a dream saying, 'Get up, take the child and his mother and go to the land of Israel. For those who were seeking the child's life are dead.' So Joseph got up, took the child and his mother and went to the land of Israel. But when he heard that Archelaus reigned over Judea in place of his father Herod, he was afraid to go there. Being warned of God in a dream, he left for the region of Galilee. He went and made his home in a city called Nazareth, so that what was spoken through the prophets might be fulfilled, 'He will be called a Nazarene.'
>
> (Matthew 2.19–23)

In these dark tales, there is a certain reassurance in the repetition Matthew employs. It reminds us of the repetition we loved in the stories we were read as children. Matthew uses exactly the same form of words to introduce the angel as he did back in verse 13, when it came to warn Joseph to escape from Bethlehem. The beginning of the angel's speech here is identical to the opening of that earlier one too, although this time its tidings are much more reassuring. Joseph's precise obedience, 'So Joseph got up, took the child and his mother,' is a repetition of the first words of verse 14. Later he is 'warned of God in a dream', just as the magi were in verse 12, and Matthew says he 'left' for the region of Galilee, just as the magi 'left' for their own country. Such repetition, clearly deliberate, gives more than reassurance; it introduces order into a chaotic world, pattern into a wild series of events, where things might seem out of control.

The angel does that, too, of course. God is still at work. He has not been thwarted. Once again he will bring good out of evil. That is what the angel both signifies and declares.

And the references to Scripture perform a similar function. The last one in the passage, to do with Jesus being a Nazarene, is somewhat mystifying. For there is no mention of Nazareth in the tradition, and if Matthew believed that somewhere in the prophets in his Scriptures (notice he seems pretty vague about it) there was a verse that did speak of it, he was mistaken. He is wrong, also, to call Nazareth a 'city'. The real Nazareth was 'a small Jewish settlement with no more than two to four hundred inhabitants' (John Dominic Crossan and Jonathan L. Reed, *Excavating Jesus*, 2001, p. 32). When Nathanael is told about Jesus in the first chapter of John's Gospel and learns he comes from Nazareth, he famously remarks, 'Can anything good come out of Nazareth?' (John 1.46). As some have commented, what is surprising is not that Nathanael should despise tiny Nazareth, but that he should have heard of it.

Yet for Matthew the family's settling in Nazareth is, like the rest, in accordance with his Scriptures and with the declared will and purpose of God. And there is another real and more significant appeal to Scripture hidden in this passage. When Matthew has the angel say, 'For those who were seeking the child's life are dead', he is using words taken from the Septuagint translation of Exodus 4.19. 'The Lord said to Moses in Midian, "Go, return to Egypt, *for all those who were seeking your life are dead.*" ' The next verse of that passage begins, 'So Moses took his wife and sons, put them on a donkey and returned to the land of Egypt.' Later in Matthew's Gospel, Jesus himself will play the part of Moses, and will deliver the great 'Sermon on the Mount', just as Moses once received the Torah, the intricacies of the mind of God, on the top of Mount Sinai in Exodus 19ff. For the moment, however, Jesus is far too small to play Moses, so Joseph will have to do it for him. Earlier, when he escaped from Bethlehem, he re-enacted the story of the ancestors of the people of Israel going down to

Egypt to find sanctuary. Now he recalls the point where Moses is sent by God back into Egypt to rescue his people, and bring them out into his promised land.

One detail Matthew does not take out of the Exodus narratives is the donkey on which Moses puts his wife and sons. Artists have produced wonderful images of the holy family's flight into Egypt, none finer than the great Rembrandt's etchings of the scene. Always Rembrandt has Mary and the child Jesus riding on a donkey, and in doing that he was only following the invariable custom. But there is no donkey in Matthew's story, either when they flee to Egypt, or when they return. Does Matthew deliberately omit mention of it? We do not know, but its absence sets our imaginations to work again, and reinforces the rigours and dangers of the two long journeys that Joseph, Mary and Jesus have to undertake. On both occasions, it seems, we have to envisage them walking on foot. With this particular coming out of Egypt, we have not left the darkness entirely behind.

That is clearer still when we recall the larger setting of Exodus 4, and when we hear of the journey to Nazareth.

In Exodus 4, when Moses is commanded to return to Egypt, that is bad news as well as good. The good news is that the pharaoh who was seeking to kill him, and from whom he once fled, is no longer a threat. The bad news is that another pharaoh has succeeded to the throne, who is little better than the first. Brutal tyranny has not departed from Egypt. Indeed, that is why Moses is being sent back, to confront the new pharaoh and demand he let God's people go. To say he will have a hard time of it once he returns is an understatement. Joseph, for his part, soon learns that though Herod is dead, his son Archelaus has come to power in Judea in his stead. The first-century Jewish historian Josephus claims that protests to Rome about Archelaus' 'cruelty and tyranny' led to his removal and exile to Gaul. Joseph does indeed have cause to be afraid. Brutal tyranny has not departed from Judea. Best to keep well clear, as the magi did, when they left for their own country.

Joseph goes right up to the far north of the country, some 85 miles from Bethlehem, to a small village no one has heard of, a nowhere place, away from the centres of power, where he hopes they will not be noticed. It is hard for those of us who live in nuclear families to catch the full force of this settling in Nazareth. We live in a mobile society, where it is normal for grown-up children to live miles from their parents, and for grandparents to be living apart, also. In the world of Joseph and Mary, however, it was the extended family that was the basic social unit, the place where security and a sense of identity and belonging was to be found. In Matthew's stories of the birth of Jesus, Joseph and Mary both come from Bethlehem. That is where their families are, and the land on which its members depend. That is where their ancestors are buried, and where the history of the families is located. To go to Nazareth is far more than going to a place where they simply have to make new friends and find out about the local shops. It is to cut themselves off from their extended families and all the kinds of support those can afford. It is to go where they have no belonging, to a small peasant village where they have no land, far from their own clans, to a very precarious existence, not unlike that of many who come as refugees to the west today, who arrive with nothing and end up selling the *Big Issue* on the streets, or much worse. This last passage in Matthew's story of the birth of Jesus has no homecoming. We have not left the darkness behind.

And Mary and Jesus remain in its shadows. If we look at the verbs in this passage, they are all in the singular. 'Get up, take . . . go' the angel says. It is speaking to Joseph, and the Greek verbs are all in the masculine singular. Then we have 'he got up, he took . . . he went . . . he heard . . . he was afraid . . . he was warned . . . he left . . . he went . . . he made his home'. The verbs make Mary and Jesus invisible. God deals, as he always has in Matthew's Scriptures, with men, not with women and children. Men have clear authority over women and children, and must take all decisions. That was the assumption in Matthew's world, and it was rarely challenged. As it turns out, as the stories of the Gospels unfold, Jesus *will* challenge it, and so will Luke, as soon we will see.

Meanwhile, Jesus has at least escaped with his life. He was not in Bethlehem when Herod's soldiers arrived with their

swords already drawn. It will not always be like that. When
Matthew reaches the climax of his Gospel and tells the story
of Jesus' arrest and trials, then Jesus will not escape the killing,
but will himself die a brutal death and will then take God into
the very heart of the darkness. But that is another story.

# 7

## *Reflections*

———•◆•———

Before we move on to Luke, let us pause for some reflection, or rather for four reflections. For 30 years, first as a school chaplain, then as a tutor in biblical studies in a theological college, and finally as a priest working in a cathedral, I have occasionally preached through storytelling or poetry. The story or poem I have written has been the sermon, and I have in each case stopped when the story or poem itself is finished. A good few of my pieces relate to the great festivals of the Christian year, especially Christmas, Good Friday and Easter. When we reach those festivals, we enter the holy of holies of our faith and its most mysterious and profound moments; we hear the beating heart of God. Sometimes I have found myself driven to using storytelling or poetry, as only one of those will allow me to begin to express what I wish to say. Over the years SPCK have published five small collections of my pieces. Of the four reflections that now follow, the first two have never before been published. The first is a poem for Advent; the three stories after it all relate closely to Matthew's narrative of Jesus' birth, but go beyond it in their reference to events or conditions of our own times, as well as to memories of my own, and in their dependence on my own free imagination.

## Waiting for God

*I preached this in Chester Cathedral on Advent Sunday 2005, relatively soon after the devastating earthquake in Kashmir – hence the reference to it in one of its lines. The Old Testament reading that day came from Isaiah and included the words, 'We are the clay, and you our potter; we are all the work of your hand' (Isaiah 64.8b,c).*

And so once more the wheel of the year has turned
and we are back at the beginning,
at this time of waiting.
Four weeks of waiting.
We have come out of the crush of Eastgate Street
and the queues at the tills,
to this place of waiting,
where we can sit and listen;
a place where the rush stops,
where the television is not switched on,
with its nervous chatter of the world's disasters
and its sorting through the pickings of our wickedness;
no e-mails can reach us here,
and if the mobile phone should ring,
then we will quickly turn it off,
our faces redder than before.
We have turned aside to this patch of holy ground
to sit and wait
at this time precisely set aside,
like Lent,
for waiting.

Four weeks now of waiting.
Four weeks!
The insistent world in which we live
would have us want things now,
with the click of a button
and the blink of an eye.
But we have turned aside to wait,
in God's good time.

So what are we waiting for?
Waiting for God to come and take us home,
to lead us up her garden path,
past trees of Wisdom and of Life,
to open wide the door,
to cheer our spirits,
chase off the gloomy clouds of night,
to close the path to misery,
put on the kettle,

sit us down to tea and cake
and make us laugh.

As darkness falls we wish to sit with her
and hear her tales,
words that will not pass away.
We want our favourite story once again,
the one we think we know so well,
of journeys and a moving star,
of a birth without pain
and a child who never cries,
of shepherds smelling of angels,
and the wisest of kings
bending low with gifts in outstretched hands
to a mother who is not tired at all,
and a man who does not mind the child is not his.
We want our make-believe.

God will tell it differently,
if only we will hear.

But that is not for now.
For now we wait, and waiting still, we wait.

Waiting for God is surely a strange occupation,
for God is all about us
in the wild skies,
the clouds unravelled by the wind,
the sun that turns the trees to gold and sea to duck-
    egg blue,
in the gorse that flowers even in the frost,
the shades of winter bracken,
the lifted wings of swans,
the cries of whiffling geese;
in the kindness of strangers,
in acts of unexpected courtesy,
in the fresh companionship of old friends,
the love of those whose wedding is near,
in the delight of small children,
and the quiet courage of the old;
in the banter of hospital wards,

in all payment of attention and all showing of care,
all understanding and forgiving,
all making of peace,
all whistle-blowing where whistles should be blown,
all standing firm for truth and striving for what is just,
all giving and acquiring of dignity
in all searching and finding of mystery,
in all humility.
We are surrounded by such a cloud of witnesses!
How can we wait for a God who has already arrived?

Because things are not all sweetness and light.
Need I spell it out?
Scratch every arm
and the blood of pain will come fast welling to the skin.
We have other tales to tell, if we dare tell them,
and we, we are not shivering in the cold of Kashmir,
nor striving to survive Mugabe's madness,
nor are we high-walled and road-blocked into
    Bethlehem.
Sometimes it seems God is more than just four weeks away.

And so we wait.
We all wait.

What picture shall we carry with us,
pack into our luggage
for this pilgrimage of Advent
(for waiting is not sitting still,
but moving on to God's own destination)?
'We are the clay, and you our potter; we are all the
    work of your hand.'
That will do.
That will do just fine.
We will imagine you,
great God of heaven and earth,
with your hands on the wheel,
holding us together,
keeping us whole,
stopping us flying off at a tangent
to land in pieces on the floor,

pressing us,
moulding us,
smoothing us,
bending us,
teasing us into shape,
then glazing us,
firing us,
holding us up for the light to catch.
This we will take on our journey,
for it brings you so near, O God
(for what could be closer than a potter to her clay?),
and we would dearly love to think of ourselves
as your fine handiwork,
and you dressed in an apron
washing dirty hands and fingernails!
Dressed like that, O God,
you will not seem out of place
when Mary's time has come and the neighbours are
    sent for.

## Joseph's story

I want to tell you how it was. As close to it as I can, at any
rate. Because you've got it wrong, got Mary and me wrong,
too. You've smothered us in piety, buried us deep in doctrine.
And you've been more concerned about your precious doctrine than about us. I want to tell you about us. I want to
make it clear. It was far more ordinary and more sordid than
you make out. But far, far more wonderful, far more extraordinary, a much greater miracle than you suppose. I still
can't take it in. Talk about good out of evil and grace out of
disgrace! God's a marvel, he is!

But I've skipped on too far. Let me go back to the beginning.

Mary and I were betrothed. Her family were pleased about
that. My family had good land and, what was more important, a good pedigree. Went back to Jesse we did, and his son
David. We had royalty in our family, we did, and against all
the odds and all the wars the centuries had seen, we were still
in Bethlehem, still with some of Jesse's fields.

So Mary's father was delighted when my father talked to him about us getting married. We solemnly agreed we would marry, in front of witnesses. Mary was 13. In a year's time the second marriage ceremony would be held, and she would join our family and we would live together. But we counted as husband and wife from that day on, though Mary still lived with her parents. I thought I would explain it. You need to understand. Mary was 13. Soon she would be able to have children.

Only she jumped the gun, as you might say. She got pregnant. It wasn't mine; I knew that. I didn't know anything else, except that all our hopes were ended. Hope itself was withered on the vine, shrivelled up, crushed into the dirt.

I tried shouting the truth out of her. She wouldn't tell me what happened. She kept her eyes on the ground and her mouth shut. 'You've ruined everything!' I told her. 'Do you realize what you've done? Do you realize the shame, the disgrace you've brought on my father, on our family, on me? You're a whore, Mary! You're soiled goods, Mary, dirty, filthy, untouchable! I'll never touch you again. I'm going to accuse you of adultery, Mary, because I can't bear the shame of it. I'll bring this shame of ours crashing down on you and your father and your family. I'll bring what you've done right out in public! You'll never live it down, Mary! Never! You'll bear it not just for a few more months, but for the rest of your life and beyond!'

Then I ran out of the village, down the hill, beyond the fields and into the desert. I left Mary in floods of tears, clutching her stomach.

I spent that night in the desert. The wadis ran with my own tears that night. And a new shame came upon me, shame for what I'd said. She was only 13. Whoever had done this must have forced her. I knew what Mary was like. I didn't need the elders of the village to conduct a trial and tell me whether she was raped or not. I knew Mary. I loved Mary. I would go to her the next day and beg her to forgive me. I would tell her I hadn't forgiven her, because there was nothing to forgive. It was not her fault. I would divorce her as quietly as I could. I would tell my father, and we'd get a couple of witnesses we could trust, and we'd hand back the marriage agreement. She'd have the baby at home, her own family's home. She would bear its curse for the rest of her life, but there was nothing I could do about that. The baby would bear her curse, also. But there was nothing I could do about that, either.

So when the sun came up the next day, I went back to the village. I told Mary all the things I'd worked out to say. Then we embraced and we cried and held on to one another for a long time. Mary knew I was right. There was nothing else to do.

I spent the next night in the desert, as well. I didn't sleep. A leopard crept silently among the rocks above me, and the ibex shifted their feet and suddenly went bounding away, sending stones spinning into the wadi. Their panic shook me out of my reverie, and I looked up and saw an angel. Well, God, really. But you're not supposed to say you've seen God.

God had Mary by the hand. That's what I saw, as clear as the stars in the desert sky. They stood there, together, looking at me, as clear and as shining as the sky turning to dawn in the east, across the Dead Sea. And as they stood there, all my shame turned to honour, the greatest honour in all the world. All our disgrace, the disgrace I'd so plainly thought disgrace, the disgrace I'd believed was so large, enough to swallow us whole, Mary and me and our families, that disgrace which a moment ago had been my world, my universe, my tomb, and Mary's too, that disgrace was turned quite all to grace. And the grace was not just ours (though it *was* ours, oh yes, it was ours!) it was grace enough for all the world, for all creation, enough to fill the universe for evermore! The child, so tiny yet, growing inside my Mary's womb was the very Love of God! It was a miracle, the biggest, finest miracle you ever did see!

That's what I saw in the desert, as clear as clear.

So I ran back to the village, and when I got to Mary I was so puffed I couldn't speak, so I held her and she held me and my joy flowed into her and her joy flowed into me and eventually, when I'd got my breath back, I told her about seeing God and her together in the desert, and she said she'd seen God, too, and I said all the disgrace had turned to grace, and she said the same, and I said it was enough to fill the world, and she said yes, and for all time, too, and we laughed and we danced and we cried and we laughed again, and of course we completed the marriage, and she came to live with me, and the child was born, and soon after that we taught the Love of God to walk.

I wish we'd all lived happily ever after. But you only get that in your fairy stories. Our story was no fairy story. It was God's story, and that's different.

## An interview with the magi

*This piece appeared in my fifth collection of stories and poems,* God Treads Softly Here, *under the title 'An interview with the wise men' (I was not so clear then about calling them magi). Not so long before I preached it in the cathedral, I had helped lead a pilgrimage to the Sinai desert, where we had met some Bedouin and once been given quiet and courteous entertainment by a man playing a simple lute. A small girl, his daughter, had curled herself in his lap. I have played with that memory, while avoiding turning the magi into Bedouin. I have altered the title of the piece, and gently edited its text.*

There was silence in the tent. The magi were sitting on an exquisite Persian carpet, perfectly still. They seemed uneasy, distracted. The Western journalist was not used to sitting on the floor, and was finding it hard to make herself comfortable. She wondered whether her gender was a problem. Indeed, she had been surprised when they had agreed to speak to her, particularly in the relative privacy of the tent. From time to time someone brought in more sweet tea for her to drink and small piles of sweet cakes.

The silence was broken by the sounds of a lute and soft singing. One of the three had taken down his lute from a peg, tuned it and started playing and singing. The other two joined in, and soon children appeared at the door of the tent, and one of them ran to the lute player and threw herself into his lap. He stopped playing and smiled down at her as she ran small fingers over the strings. The lilting song continued, and soon the small child was asleep. The man stroked her head. The other two watched him. All three had tears in their eyes.

The lute player spoke first:

| | |
|---|---|
| *1st magus* | Sometimes we wish we hadn't gone. |
| *2nd magus* | Often. |
| *3rd magus* | We were fools. |
| *1st magus* | Impossibly naïve. |

Silence came once more. The child lay fast asleep in the man's arms.

| | |
|---|---|
| *Journalist* | What do you mean? You found what you were searching for. |
| *3rd magus* | Do you not know what happened after we left for home? |
| *Journalist* | You mean the slaughter of the children? |
| *1st magus* | The massacre, yes. They were smaller than little Vashti here. We could have prevented it. |
| *Journalist* | By going back to Herod and telling him exactly where he could find Jesus, do you mean? Surely you couldn't have done that? |
| *3rd magus* | No, of course, we couldn't. We didn't belong to Herod's secret police. And in any case after we had seen that child, nothing on earth would have made us betray him. If Herod had captured us and tortured us, he would have got nothing out of us. |
| *2nd magus* | But we shouldn't have blundered into Jerusalem asking for the King of the Jews. We should have asked if they had a king already. Two kings for one throne is one too many. We knew that, of course. But we assumed when we saw this new king's star that the old king must be dead. We were wrong, quite tragically so. |
| *1st magus* | We should have asked more questions first. We should have found out about Herod. |
| *3rd magus* | And we shouldn't have been beguiled by the temple he was building. It was the grandest thing we had ever seen. On such a scale! Such fine workmanship! The blocks of stone so finely cut! We had heard tales of Persepolis, once the royal centre of our empire, with its palaces |

|              | and irrigated gardens. Jerusalem reminded us of those old stories. A palace for its god, set on a huge platform, so the whole world could come and fall at his feet. |
| *2nd magus* | And pay homage to the king who had built it for him. |
| *Journalist* | What do you mean the temple 'beguiled' you? |
| *2nd magus* | It led us to expect the wrong kind of king, and to think our gifts were appropriate. We had gold and frankincense and myrrh in our saddlebags. We imagined we would find the new king in a splendid court, surrounded by his slaves and guarded by soldiers. So we had brought presents fit for such a monarch. That was stupid. |
| *1st magus* | Yet not nearly so stupid as the question we asked in the suq in Jerusalem. 'Where is the new-born king of the Jews,' we said. 'For we saw his star rise in the night sky back in Persia,' we said. 'We set out to follow it, and here we are,' we said. Such fools! Why couldn't we have kept our mouths shut, been more discreet, more wise? The children of Bethlehem would not then have died. |

He turned his face away. His tears fell on Vashti's face. Gently he wiped them away with his sleeve.

| *1st magus* | When after our audience with Herod . . . |

He looked down and shook his head. There was a long silence. Eventually he picked up the story again.

|              | After our audience with Herod we rode the few miles to Bethlehem and found the child king we had come for. Or rather, we found something, someone quite different. |
| *2nd magus* | We had turned our backs on Herod's temple. We found no court, no slaves, no soldiers at |

our destination. Instead we found a peasant family's house, with its space for their two animals, and a peasant family's hospitality, and a young girl and her husband and a child crying for milk, and the whole of heaven squeezed in among them all. We were embarrassed about the gifts we had brought. They seemed at first quite out of place, far too grand, far too expensive and exclusive. Yet they were at once accepted. We had brought the finest things we could think of, and they were placed carefully among the gifts the rest of the village had brought, including the children. They too had brought their finest things.

*1st magus*  We had not found a king. We had found a God, and that was quite different. We are so glad we went. How could we not be? And yet . . .

*2nd magus*  The God-child had to escape to Egypt after we had gone. Did you know that? They left their families behind. Did you know that? And did you know that Mary's sister had her own baby, a few weeks old, and Joseph's brother a small boy just starting to walk?

*3rd magus*  That is why we and our wives and children now run this orphanage.

The interviewer looked across to the entrance of the tent. The children were still standing there, looking at her.

The first magus pointed to Vashti sleeping in his arms. Then he beckoned to them, and at once they ran in and flung themselves upon the other two magi and upon the journalist, until they were quite buried in a giggling heap of small bodies.

Vashti slept through it all.

## The soldier's tale

*A few years ago I wrote this story and three others for a Christmastide service in the cathedral. Like those other three it is to be found in my third collection of stories and poems,*

**The Three Faces of Christ.** *I have given Matthew's story of the massacre of the children of Bethlehem a contemporary setting, and towards the end made use of an account I had read of an incident which had happened shortly before in the West Bank town of Ramallah. I have kept faithfully to the details of that account. With the rest, however, I have made very free use of my imagination.*

I won't keep you long. I've plenty to tell, but I can't bear to think of the words for most of it.

We were only obeying orders. We were at the end of a long chain of command. The wrong end.

Killing children is not all that peculiar. We weren't the first, and weren't the last, either. Jericho, Auschwitz, Cambodia, Bosnia, Rwanda . . . Bethlehem. It's all the same. Except that we were told to leave the adults alone and any children over three. The other places were worse than that, and the killers weren't so choosy.

Some of us got quietly drunk before we started. The only way we could cope. We had orders only to take the little ones, as I've said, though we had to give some of the women a right beating to get their babies from them and get them off our backs.

When we'd finished, they loaded us into trucks to take us back to Jerusalem. I was dead lucky. They put me in the last one, right at the back of the convoy. Halfway back I jumped out. The others didn't move. 'Good luck', the corporal said, gave me a bit of a shove, and that was that.

I knew the lie of the land. I'd been brought up nearby, see. The desert was close. They'd never find me there, I thought. I knew some of the Bedouin. They'd give me shelter and a change of clothes, and enough food and drink to get me to the border.

They did too. Then the rains came in buckets in the hills, and the wadis got full of water. When I climbed down into one, I'd strip off my clothes and wash myself all over. But I could never get myself clean. It felt as though the blood of those babies had soaked right through my skin, and I'd have it all dark and spoiled inside me till the day I died.

Still, after a bit I made it to Egypt. I tried to disappear, but the faces of those babies still followed me. In the end I couldn't take it any more, so I decided to go back and give myself up.

On the way I bumped into a young woman and her husband. They had a child with them. He was very small, still a baby really. I couldn't keep my eyes off him, though God knows I tried.

'Where are you from?' I asked.

'We had to escape from Bethlehem a while ago,' they said. 'There was a terrible massacre. All the children under three, killed. Can you imagine? We got out by the skin of our teeth. We're not going back. Going up north instead, to Nazareth.'

They saw me looking at the baby and noticed the expression on my face. The mother hesitated. She suddenly realized I'd been a part of it. I'm sure she did. But then she said (you won't believe this), 'Do you want to hold him for a moment?' And before I could say anything, she put him in my arms.

So many of us deserted after the massacre, they've stopped looking for us. Least, that's what people say. I work in Ramallah now, an Arab place north of Jerusalem. There was trouble in the town the other day. I expect you read about it in the newspapers. Some things they didn't tell you, though. The soldiers were using high-velocity bullets that explode inside you. See this scar? A doctor and I were bending over someone who'd been shot. He was bleeding heavily. We were right inside a room on the fifth floor of a block of flats. The soldiers must've been using telescopic sights, and they can't have missed our uniforms. We were wearing white coats, after all. But they shot at us all the same. One of the bullets hit the doctor smack in the head. I just got shrapnel in the back and in my shoulder. Another team went up for the man we'd been trying to help, and somehow they managed to get him out, and the doctor and me as well. The man's still alive. The doctor isn't, of course.

I will work for justice until I die. That baby on the road from Egypt, and his mother, they showed me what I had to do. Showed me I was forgiven, too. I could feel it strong, when she handed him to me and I held him in my arms. It was like holding the fire of God.

# 8

## An angel, a priest, and a woman who loses her 'disgrace'

—◆◆◆—

'In the sixth month the angel Gabriel was sent from God to a town in Galilee called Nazareth, to a virgin betrothed to a man whose name was Joseph, of the house of David. The virgin's name was Mary.' We only have to hear those words to be transported into another world, a world of candles and bells, carols and organs going full blast, and turkey and mince pies and presents under the tree.

Yet this is not how the story of Jesus' birth begins in Luke. The exquisite story of the annunciation to Mary is not the first in his Gospel. The narrative of the birth of Jesus is entwined with another, the tale of the birth of John the Baptist. After a short, formal prologue, Luke has this:

> In the days of Herod king of Judea, there was a priest named Zechariah, who belonged to the priestly order of Abijah. His wife was a descendant of Aaron, and her name was Elizabeth. Both of them were righteous before God, living according to all the commandments and ordinances of the Lord, blameless. But they had no child, for Elizabeth was barren, and both were getting on in years.
>
> Once when he was serving as priest before God and his section was on duty, he was chosen by lot, according to the custom of the priesthood, to enter the sanctuary of the Lord and offer incense. Now at the time of the incense offering, the whole assembly of the people was praying outside. Then there appeared to him an angel of the Lord, standing at the right side of the altar of incense. When Zechariah saw him he was scared out of his wits,

The Christmas Stories

and fear overwhelmed him. But the angel said to him, 'Do not be afraid, Zechariah, for your prayer has been heard. Your wife Elizabeth will bear you a son, and you will name him John. You will have joy and gladness, and many will rejoice at his birth, for he will be great in the sight of the Lord. He must never drink wine or strong drink; he will be filled with the Holy Spirit even while he is in his mother's womb. He will turn many of the people of Israel to the Lord their God. With the spirit and power of Elijah he will go before him, to turn the hearts of fathers to their children, and the disobedient to the wisdom of the righteous, to make ready a people prepared for the Lord.' Zechariah said to the angel, 'How will I know that this is so? For I am an old man and my wife is getting on in years.' The angel replied and said to him, 'I am Gabriel. I stand in the presence of God, and I have been sent to speak to you and to bring you these glad tidings. Now behold, because you did not believe my words, which will be fulfilled in their time, you will be mute, unable to speak, until the day these things occur.'

Meanwhile the people were waiting for Zechariah, and were amazed that he was spending so much time inside the sanctuary. When he did come out, he could not speak to them, and they realized he had seen a vision in the sanctuary. He kept beckoning to them, but he remained speechless. When his days of service were completed, he went back to his home.

After those days his wife Elizabeth conceived, and for five months she hid herself. She said, 'This is what the Lord has done for me when he looked favourably on me and took away the disgrace I have endured among my people.'                                    (Luke 1.5–25)

'In the days of Herod king of Judea,' it begins. Ominous words indeed, to us who have just come from Matthew's story of the massacre of all those babies and young children. But this is Luke, not Matthew. Mercifully Herod will play no part in his stories of the birth of Jesus. If his opening is more than a chronological marker, then it acts as a reminder to the hearers

68

and readers of his Gospel that they are back in a time when the temple at Jerusalem was still in place, indeed was being built. By the time Luke wrote it had been destroyed by the Romans. His words also link his narrative with the books of the prophets in his Jewish Scriptures, for the books of Isaiah, Jeremiah, Hosea, Amos, Micah and Zephaniah all begin by locating the words of the prophets in the time of such and such a king, or kings. This kind of echo is far from accidental. The two opening chapters of Luke, with which we will be concerned, are soaked in the Jewish Scriptures, the stories of the births of John and Jesus marinated in the ancient sacred tales of the Jewish people. Only twice, in the story of the presentation of Jesus in the temple, will Luke actually quote the biblical text, and that will be only to make clear that Mary and Joseph were complying with the requirements of the Jewish Torah. Yet, to use musical parlance, we might call every passage of these birth narratives a variation on a biblical theme, a playing with the storytelling and poetry of the Jewish Scriptures. Luke himself obviously knew them inside out, and he expects his hearers and readers to hear the echoes of their many voices in the new story he has to tell. As we ourselves try to listen to his tales, we will draw attention to some of the more significant ones.

Luke's story of the birth of Jesus begins and ends in the Jewish temple. One day that same temple will be Jesus' undoing. He will cause mayhem there such as the temple authorities cannot ignore, and they will be out for his blood (Luke 19.45–47). Jesus will pronounce the temple's imminent destruction, 'when not one stone will be left upon another' (21.6), a time when 'Jerusalem will be trampled on by the Gentiles' (21.24b). But these opening chapters blaze with light and hope, and the temple means here a place where truly God is found and where God's will is done. It means what it was for almost all Jews at the time of its existence, the very heart of their faith, the visible sign of God's presence, the sign that their God was with them, sharing in their journey, even if the old tent of meeting of the book of Exodus had become something too large and heavy for even God to place upon his shoulder.

The temple was a vast complex, with courtyards for Gentiles, women and Jewish men. Almost all its ceremony and its business of sacrifice and prayer were conducted in those courtyards, in the open air. Only the priests themselves were allowed inside the sanctuary itself, and the opportunity for them to do so would arise very seldom. There were so many priests that each order or division of them would serve at the temple only for two separate weeks in the year. Incense was burned in the sanctuary before the morning sacrifices, and again after the evening ones were finished. The five priests required for the task were chosen not on a strict rota basis, but by the casting of lots; a means, so it was believed, of gaining access to the mind and choice of God, and avoiding the possibility of human corruption. Zechariah is an old man, and has been acting as a priest for very many years, but this is perhaps the first time he has been chosen for this duty. It represents for him a singular honour, the most solemn moment perhaps of his whole life. He will enter the sanctuary, offer up the prayers of the people, and then will emerge to bless the crowd outside with the ancient and beautiful priestly blessing: 'The LORD bless you and keep you; the LORD make his face to shine upon you, and be gracious to you; the LORD lift up his countenance upon you, and give you peace' (Numbers 6.24–26). Twenty years ago I myself was once in a synagogue in Jerusalem for the Sabbath morning service, when 'the sons of Aaron', those who counted themselves as the descendants of the old priests of the temple, stood on a high platform in front of the ark containing the sacred scrolls, drew their prayer shawls over their heads and chanted those words from Numbers. I have never forgotten it and never will. It was truly a moment of blessing.

Yet Zechariah's wildest dreams will not touch what awaits him inside the sanctuary. Before him is the curtained door leading to the Holy of Holies, where the glory of God is focused down to a few square feet. He is not allowed to go through that, only the high priest, and he but once a year on the Day of Atonement. But Zechariah does not need to go there, for heaven, in the guise of the angel Gabriel, steps out of hiding to meet him, and surrounds him with more glory than he can take.

He is terrified, as so many in the Bible are when they encounter the divine. Yet at once the angel tries to calm his fear: 'Do not be afraid,' he says. That is a mark of the speech of God. It is the most common saying in the Bible, and again and again we find it in the mouth of God or of one who comes from his divinity. Christians have often turned God into a figure who is very frightening indeed, and we often still do. Against us those words are spoken, over and over, 'Do not fear; do not be afraid.'

This time it is, 'Do not be afraid, Zechariah, for your prayer has been heard. Your wife Elizabeth will bear you a son.' 'So *that* is what Zechariah has been praying for,' we say. 'He should have been offering up the prayers of the people.' In fact it seems he has, for he reacts to Gabriel's promise of a son with complete incredulity, as if he stopped praying for a child and gave up hope of one long ago. His priesthood is hereditary. He inherited it from his father and he needs a son to whom he can pass it on. Elizabeth is the daughter of a priest, also. She is a descendant of Aaron, as he is. But without a son, the priestly line that stretches down to them both will end. Gabriel promises him precisely what he has *not* been praying for, not for a long time. But once he did. And so did Elizabeth. Any woman in her position would have done, and her own response, given at the very end of this passage, surely comes from years not only of longing, but of praying.

Zechariah's incomprehension is perfectly understandable, of course. This may be storytelling, but there is a limit to the extent Luke, or Gabriel for that matter, can suspend our disbelief, or Zechariah's. The idea of Elizabeth conceiving a son is indeed quite impossible. They are both simply too old. But the promise, and his response to it, put Zechariah, and Elizabeth too, in very good company. The book of Genesis, after its long prologue (chapters 1–11), is concerned with a single family, the ancestors of the people of Israel. It covers four generations, and the first three of them have a problem with fertility or, as Genesis puts it, with barren women. (When a couple do not have children, the Bible always blames the woman. It is never a case of the husband's sperm count.) When Sarah, Abraham's wife is introduced to us, we learn at once she is barren (Genesis 11.29–30). Eventually Isaac is born and later marries Rebekah, and then finds himself praying to God for a child because she is barren (Genesis 25.21). Isaac's son, Jacob, marries two women, Leah and Rachel. He is married to Leah only through a trick, and Rachel is the one he loves. And she too is barren. Only after the still unloved Leah has given birth to six sons and a daughter does Rachel have a son: 'And God remembered Rachel and God heard her and he opened her womb, and she conceived and bore a son, and she said, "God has taken away my shame."' (Genesis 30.22–23, Robert Alter's translation, *The Five Books of Moses*, 1995, p. 162). That son is Joseph, the one destined to become centre stage for the last quarter of the book.

Luke in his story of Zechariah and Elizabeth has picked elements from the stories of all three of those 'barren' women. Zechariah has been praying for a son, as Isaac did (and Abraham, also – see Genesis 15.2–3); Elizabeth's response echoes Rachel's when her Joseph is born; and Zechariah's and Elizabeth's old age, and his bewilderment remind us at once of Abraham and Sarah. There were yet more stories of barren women in Luke's mind when he wrote this chapter, particularly those of Eluma, the rabbi-named wife of Manoah, in the wonderfully funny and subversive tale of the birth of Samson in Judges 13, and of Hannah in 1 Samuel 1, who after years of agonizing childlessness, brings Samuel to birth. When Gabriel announces that Zechariah's and Elizabeth's child must never have wine or strong drink, that echoes the instructions Eluma receives in her encounter with heaven (see Judges 13.4, 7, 14). And Hannah's tale will soon come to prominence, when later in Luke 1 we come to Mary and her famous song. For now, however, it is chiefly Abraham and Sarah that Luke would have us remember. For Abraham, we learn from Genesis 17.17, is 100 years old when Isaac is born, and Sarah 90! She is long past the menopause and they have long given up having sexual intercourse (Genesis 18.11–12). Abraham thinks the idea of them having a child ridiculous (17.17), and so does Sarah, who cannot hide her laughter (18.12–13).

Coming from Genesis 17–18 to Luke's story of the meeting in the temple, we might think Gabriel's response to Zechariah more than a little harsh. Sarah is (unfairly) told off by God for laughing (Genesis 18.13–14), but receives no further punishment, while Abraham receives not even a rebuke, although his laughter comes close to mockery and blasphemy, since he is prostrate before his God at the time, in the attitude of worship and obedience (Genesis 17.17 begins, 'Then Abraham fell on his face and laughed'). Zechariah's being struck dumb means he will not be able to utter those words from Numbers 6. He will not be able to bless the people, as is his privilege and his duty. And this when he is such a good man, too. Abraham in Genesis is not. He has his magnificent moment or two, but in the Genesis tales he is a deeply flawed human being, and towards Sarah is cowardly, unfeeling and selfish. Zechariah is introduced as an exemplary character, as is Elizabeth. You cannot get any better in the Bible than the way they are introduced to us in Luke 1.6. When Job is said to be 'blameless, upright, God-fearing, *and* one who shuns evil', that is over the top, deliberate parody. The best people in the Bible usually only get one or two stars. It is a rare person indeed who is awarded three. Noah, the only good person in a violent world, we are told, gets three (see Genesis 6.5–9). Zechariah and Elizabeth get three.

Elizabeth, however, does not laugh, except, no doubt, with joy. By the tenets of Jewish piety, her response remains exemplary. Quite why she hides herself away for five months is not clear. At least that means that when she does emerge the pregnancy is fairly secure and obvious to all who see her. Now she can walk the streets of her town with more than a smile on her face, and all will be able to see that indeed her 'disgrace' has been taken away.

We may balk at the word 'disgrace' but, given the beliefs and assumptions of Elizabeth's day, it is all too readily understandable. Of course, in our own times many women who do not conceive blame themselves and think they have let their husbands or partners down. They will find it easy to begin to enter Elizabeth's world. But only to begin, for now we understand so much more about the processes of human conception and about what can hinder them. And most of us are not burdened with the darker side of Elizabeth's theology.

In the Jewish Scriptures each and every birth is a mystery and a sign of God's creative activity. In the Garden of Eden story, as early as Genesis 2–3, we are given a delicate and mysterious account of the making of the first human beings, where the language is freighted with God's intimacy, and tells of the strange and wonderful dignity of these new creatures. Elsewhere God is sometimes compared to a father, or mother, or midwife, and each and every child is regarded as a gift of God, an expression of his blessing. The question of a pregnancy or birth that is unwanted is never raised, despite there being no reliable contraception. The poet of Psalm 139 expresses most beautifully the sense of wonder that filled the minds of those who contemplated the mystery of the growth of the foetus in the womb. The words are addressed to God.

> For it was you who formed my inward parts;
> you knit me together in my mother's womb.
> I praise you, for I am fearfully and wonderfully made.
> Wonderful are your works;
> that I know very well.
> My frame was not hidden from you,
> when I was being made in secret,
> intricately woven in the depths of the earth.
> Your eyes beheld my unformed substance.
> In your book were written
> all the days that were formed for me,
> when none of them as yet existed.
> How weighty to me are your thoughts, O God!
> How vast is the sum of them!
>
> (Psalms 139.13–17)

A bewildered and deeply hurt Job asks God to explain why he is tormenting him, when he took such care over the making of him:

> Your hands fashioned and made me ...
> Remember that you fashioned me like clay ...
> Did you not pour me out like milk
> and curdle me like cheese?

You clothed me with skin and flesh,
and knit me together with bones and sinews.
You have granted me life and steadfast love,
and your care has preserved my spirit.

(Job 10.8a, 9a, 10–12)

When Rachel conceives Joseph, the text of Genesis reads, 'Then God remembered Rachel and God heeded her and opened her womb' (30.22).

But there was another side to this coin. If a married woman did not conceive, if she did not have a child, if especially she did not have a son, then that could easily be seen as some kind of punishment from God and a sign that she was not in God's favour or within the shine of his blessing: her fault lay not so much with her ovaries as with her relationship with God.

That is not the case with Elizabeth. Luke makes that plain when he first speaks of her, calling her 'righteous before God, living according to all the commandments and ordinances of the Lord, blameless'. So her inability to conceive is left as a mystery. But not to her neighbours, it seems, or members of Zechariah's or her own family. To them it is her 'disgrace', and for years she has been bearing its load.

It is not only Elizabeth's difficulty in conceiving that is left unexplained. So is the how of her conceiving. Nowhere does Luke suggest that it happens but through the normal processes of sexual intercourse. But how is it that she and Zechariah have a child when they are so old? That is not just our question, but Zechariah's too. Gabriel does not give him an answer. 'I am Gabriel. I stand in the presence of God.' The answer lies hidden in the presence of God, it seems, and even Gabriel does not know what it is, or else is not telling. A story about God must, I suppose, preserve a sense of mystery, or else it is not a story about God.

The biblical stories of once barren women conceiving are all concerned with children of very special significance for the larger purposes of God: Isaac, Jacob and Esau, Joseph and later Benjamin, Samson, Samuel. And now, John the Baptist. In the end the problems the mothers of these children experience are meant to underline the singularly creative power of the God who gives them a child, and to put that child in the brightest spotlight of God's care and attention. Near the beginning of the book of Jeremiah these words are put in the mouth of God:

> Before I formed you in the womb I knew you,
> and before you were born I consecrated you;
> I appointed you a prophet to the nations.
>
> (Jeremiah 1.5)

As Gabriel explains to Zechariah in Luke's passage, the role their child John will play when he grows up will be of huge significance.

We are here on the cusp of a new era, when God will come out of hiding.

# 9

## *Annunciation*

———◆◆◆———

The last passage began in the Jerusalem temple, inside its sanctuary, with an angel appearing to a man. It ended in a house in the hill country of Judea (see 1.39), and with a woman. The scene of our new passage is another house, its concern with another woman. And if, after Matthew's stories of the appearances of an angel to Joseph, and Luke's tale of Zechariah's meeting with Gabriel, we think that angels do not speak to women, we are about to be proved wrong.

> In the sixth month the angel Gabriel was sent from God to a town in Galilee called Nazareth, to a virgin betrothed to a man whose name was Joseph, of the house of David. The virgin's name was Mary. (1.26–27)

What now? It is the sixth month of Elizabeth's pregnancy, a few weeks since she has come out into the open and a wonder of God's doing is plain for all to see in the unexpected curve of her belly. Will there now be a greater wonder still? Will God himself come further out of hiding? Of course. Storytellers work with crescendos. It is unthinkable that Luke will speak of something less remarkable than John's conception, or merely equal to it. Is there already a hint of the greater miracle to come in Mary's being twice described as a virgin? Yes, there is.

> And he entered and said, 'Rejoice, most favoured one! The Lord is with you.' But she was terrified and tried to work out what sort of greeting this could be. The angel said to her, 'Do not be afraid, Mary, for you have found favour with God. Behold, you will conceive in your womb and will give birth to a son and will call him Jesus.

He will be great and will be called the Son of the Most
High, and the Lord God will give him the throne of his
ancestor David. He will reign over the house of Jacob
forever, and of his kingdom there will be no end.' Mary
said to the angel, 'How will this be, since I have no relations with a man?' The angel answered her and said to
her, 'The Holy Spirit will come upon you and the power
of the Most High will overshadow you; therefore the
child to be born will be holy; he will be called Son of
God. And behold, your relative Elizabeth in her old age
has herself conceived a son, and this is the sixth month
for her who was called barren. For nothing will be
impossible with God.' Then Mary said, 'Behold the Lord's
slave! Let it be with me according to your word.' And the
angel departed from her.                          (1.28–38)

This passage has inspired some of the most beautiful paintings in Western art. It is not surprising. It is for many reasons
a stunning piece of writing. Yet it does not depict Mary as
usually she has been painted. As we explained in Chapter 4,
we must think of Mary being between 12 and 15. She is
Jewish and has a skin more brown than pink. She comes from
a small peasant village, where the archaeologists have found
no evidence of any public buildings, nor unearthed any fine
wares, but found only locally made pottery, grinding stones
and simple household items. Where the meeting with Gabriel
takes place is not explained, but Luke says the angel 'entered',
so we must presume we are indoors, and in Mary's home. Is
anyone else there? We do not know. In Zechariah's case, he
would have been accompanied by four other priests, but we
wouldn't know that from Luke's story. They are entirely invisible, for the simple reason they are irrelevant to the story. So
now, for the purposes of this second annunciation, Mary and
Gabriel are effectively alone, and the focus is entirely upon
them. Is Mary awake, or asleep? In Matthew, Joseph is always
asleep when the angel appears, and so are the magi, when God
warns them to go home by another route. But Zechariah was
awake when he met Gabriel and, now we are in Nazareth,
there is no mention of Mary dreaming.

How are we to understand such an experience? The short, and perhaps the long answer, too, is that we are not meant to understand. The divine is not open to analysis. The divine is to be encountered and enjoyed. We must simply step into the world created here by Luke, ready to be surprised.

The timing of the angel's visit is the same as in Matthew, between betrothal and the completion of the marriage. Mary and Joseph are not yet living together, although they count as husband and wife; as in Matthew, they are not having sexual relations with one another, for those can begin only after Mary is taken to Joseph's family home.

The angel enters without knocking. No wonder Mary is terrified – the Greek word used is surely stronger than the 'she was much perplexed' of some translations. In a remarkable drawing of the scene Rembrandt shows Mary fainting with shock and sliding off her chair, with Gabriel having to catch her to stop her falling on the floor. It was surprising enough for Zechariah when the curtain of the Holy of Holies bent aside and an angel came and stood beside the altar of incense. But that was Jerusalem and the temple and the sanctuary, the place above all places where one might expect to meet with God. This is Nazareth and an unpretentious family home. Yet still Mary is suddenly, without warning, on holy ground, near the very heart of God. The temple and all such places are put into perspective here. God does not need designated holy space to be holy, nor any grandeur or ceremony on which to take his stand. God is God and free of our machinations and expectations, able to make the ordinary quite extraordinary simply by the shadow of an angel's wing.

Gabriel tries to comfort Mary in her shock and remove her fear. 'Do not be afraid,' he says – God's usual way of talking. 'You have found favour with God,' he says. He has already called her 'most favoured one'. That is reassurance indeed, of course. Later Mary will proclaim herself 'God's slave'. Gabriel is already talking to her as if she is a member of God's household. 'Your master is mighty pleased with you,' he tells her. To which Mary might say, 'What have I done to deserve that?' She was perplexed enough by his initial greeting. So now he explains what God's favour means, the special task God has in mind for her. She will have a son who will be called, quite rightly, the Son of the Most High.

How are we to hear her response to the news? With what tone will we pronounce her words, 'How will this be, since I have no relations with a man?' Certainly there is bewilderment, and that is significant. For Mary clearly does not understand Gabriel to mean that she and Joseph will have a son once the marriage has been completed. Plainly she realizes that the announced pregnancy is to be very imminent. But that makes no sense to her. She and Joseph are firmly committed to having no sexual relations while they are only betrothed, and she cannot dream of either of them breaking that commitment. The completion of the marriage is still some time away. We have to presume all that, for otherwise her question to the angel makes no sense. I myself find more than bewilderment here. I catch raw fear, the fear of a young girl who is being told, or so she understands, that she will lose her virginity to another man. Her marriage to Joseph will be all ruined. It does not matter a fig that her child will be the Son of the Most High! How will she lose her virginity? That is what she wants to know. And who will take it away from her? She will not give it away, so some man will have to seize it. 'How will this be?' she cries.

But Zechariah failed to get a straight answer from Gabriel, and Mary does no better. 'Don't worry,' he tells her. 'God's Spirit will give you all the strength you need. God will protect you.' That is how I understand the angel's words, and if I am right, then again he sidesteps an awkward question, and leaves the how of Mary's conception a mystery. Of course, many would disagree with that. Ignoring Gabriel's obvious lack of a straight answer in the temple scene, and forgetting the teasing ambiguities, the playfulness of storytelling of this quality, they presume he is being straightforward with Mary. Whether or not they interpret this point in the story as the moment of Mary's impregnation, they claim that Gabriel means her child will come straight from heaven, direct from the Spirit of God, and that her virginity will remain intact. Yet that is not what Gabriel's words suggest.

At the beginning of Acts, Luke has the risen Jesus declare to his followers, 'You will receive power when the Holy Spirit has come upon you; and you will be my witnesses in Jerusalem, in all Judea and Samaria, and to the ends of the earth.' (Acts 1.8). That verse is foreshadowed here in Mary's annunciation scene, near the start of the Gospel, the first part of Luke's two-volume masterpiece. The resurrection stories are tales of encounter with the divine. So here in Nazareth heaven has stepped into Mary's house. The followers of Jesus in Acts are to be empowered by the Spirit of God to bear witness to Jesus, to do his work, to enlarge God's kingdom to the ends of the earth. Here Mary is promised the strength to become a loyal disciple, to do the work of God and bear witness to God's goodness and creativity. She will declare herself God's slave, and soon she will be singing a triumphant song of praise, a celebration of the work of God that for Luke will form a benchmark by which all other responses to Jesus will be judged. Luke is putting Mary on a high pedestal here, presenting her to us as the model disciple, a model for men as much as for women.

The word 'overshadow' occurs again in the Gospel itself, in the course of Luke's version of the transfiguration. That is another episode where the veil is drawn apart, where we and the three disciples who accompany Jesus to the top of the mountain are given a glimpse of heaven. It is another story of encounter with the divine. Luke writes: 'a cloud came and overshadowed them; and they were terrified as they entered the cloud. Then from the cloud came a voice that said, "This is my Son, my Chosen; listen to him!"' (Luke 9.34–35). The image of the cloud is drawn from Luke's Scriptures, where it is a common image for the presence of God. We find it in many places in Exodus to Deuteronomy, in the Psalms and the prophets, and occasionally in the historical books. No wonder the three disciples are afraid as they 'enter the cloud'. They are very close to God, and being close to God in the Bible invariably provokes an initial fear, as we have already seen. But the word 'overshadow' belongs to the reassurance that follows the fear. It reminds us, for example, of the opening verse of Psalm 57:

> Be merciful to me, O God, be merciful to me,
> for in you my soul takes refuge;

in the shadow of your wings I will take refuge,
until the destroying storms pass by.

Surely one of the most beautiful verses in the Psalms is Psalm
17.8:

Guard me as the apple of the eye;
hide me in the shadow of your wings.

Always in the Hebrew Bible, talk of God 'overshadowing' anyone signifies protection. God's shadow is never sinister, or
threatening, but warm and comforting, like the deep shadow
of the body of a mother bird brooding her young, protecting
them from the cold, the heat and the wet, allowing them to
grow and eventually come to the freedom of the air. In the
Rembrandt drawing of the annunciation I mentioned earlier
the artist depicts one of Gabriel's wings arching over Mary's
head and beginning to curl around her, like a comforting arm
about her shoulder.

So when Gabriel speaks of the Spirit of God 'coming upon'
Mary, and the power of the Most High 'overshadowing' her,
his words do not carry any sexual connotations. He does not
use the language of impregnation, but of empowerment and
protection. But given the nature of Mary's fear, Gabriel does
not count on his words giving sufficient reassurance by themselves. And so he tells her of Elizabeth and her pregnancy,
and he takes Mary back to the story of Sarah overhearing the
news that she will have a child, where the God-in-disguise tells
Abraham, 'Is anything too wonderful for the LORD?' (Genesis
18.14). That is enough. 'Behold the Lord's slave!' Mary cries,
'Let it be with me according to your word.'

It is hard to hear the voice of Mary here above the insistent clamour of the theologians and the artists over the centuries, who have wished to stress Mary's subservience to the
will of God. Their reasons for doing that are suspect, particularly in the case of the theologians – the artists have generally only reflected what they were taught by the Church and
what they knew their ecclesiastical patrons expected. Too often
the leaders of the Church have used Mary as a model of subservience in order to encourage a similar obedience from the

laity, and particularly women. They have bowed Mary's head, filled her voice with a quiet deference, and have had her say in hushed and awed tones, 'Behold the handmaid of the Lord; be it unto me according to thy word.' They have used this young girl to encourage belief in a God who demands complete obedience, and in a Church which demands the same.

Yet if again we return to the Jewish Scriptures on which these chapters of Luke depend in such large measure, we find that Mary puts herself in exalted company. For Abraham is described as God's 'slave' in Psalm 105.42, Moses in Malachi 4.4, Joshua in Joshua 24.29 and Judges 2.8, David in Ezekiel 34.23; 37.24 and Psalm 89.3, the prophets in 2 Kings 17.23, the people of God (personified as Jacob) in Isaiah 48.20, and a woman, Hannah, in 1 Samuel 1.11. We may still not like the term 'slave'. 'God treats us as his children,' you might say, 'as members of the family. God sets us free and gives us a new dignity and status. He calls us his "friends", and sits us down in his circle to eat with him. To God all slavery is abhorrent.' I could not agree more, and one of my favourite verses in the entire Bible is Exodus 33.11, where we learn that 'The LORD used to speak to Moses face to face, as one speaks to a friend.' And yet we have to remember that in the world of the Bible some slaves were highly respected and extremely powerful, none more so than some of the 'slaves' of the Roman emperor at the time of Luke, who acted as his civil servants and helped him run his empire. When Mary calls herself a 'slave' of God, we should not see her touching her forelock with a whispered, still frightened obedience. We should imagine her pulling herself up to her full height, and saying defiantly, 'Never mind the Roman emperor! I'm too good for him! I belong to God's household, now! It is God's work I am about to do, and he has given me the strength and the authority to do it! And do you know what that work is? To bring to birth God's Son, a king whose kingdom will never end! When you, Mr Emperor, are long gone, God's Son, my son, will still be on God's throne!'

There *is* obedience here, of course, a coming to terms with the astonishing task that Gabriel has announced for her, a rare maturity for one so young, and an even rarer courage. Later in Luke's Gospel her son will echo her words 'Let it be with me according to your word.' In the Garden of Gethsemane, when Jesus knows the authorities are out to get him, and his arrest is very close, he prays, 'Father, if you are willing, remove this cup from me; yet, not my will but yours be done' (22.42). Like mother, like son.

And what is Mary consenting to in this annunciation scene? She does not know, for Gabriel has not answered her question. How she will conceive her child he has not told her. She commits herself to an uncertain future, an imminent future still charged with threat of violence and disgrace, as it will be for her son in Gethsemane. But she carries with her the promise of God's warm and intimate protection, the assurance of God's own strength, and a new membership card declaring her a member of God's household. That will be enough.

The disconcerting ambiguities and obscurities of Luke's narrative have still left this young girl Mary as a profoundly inspiring and challenging figure.

# 10

## *Two women and a song*

The next passage brings Elizabeth and Mary together. It is a tale of two women, and they occupy the entire stage. Such stories are extremely rare in the Bible, and there are no others to compare with it in the New Testament. In the Old one thinks of Sarah and Hagar in Genesis 16 and 21, or Rachel and Leah in Genesis 29 and 30, or Hannah and Peninnah in 1 Samuel 1. As we have already seen, each of those cases concerns questions of fertility and barrenness, but the dissimilarities between them and the story of Elizabeth and Mary are sharp. Hagar is Sarah's rival (at least, that is how Sarah perceives and treats her), Rachel and Leah vie with one another for Jacob's affections and for the 'honour' of bearing him children, while Peninnah's repeated taunts reduce Hannah to tears. They are poignant stories, full of pain and hurt, and for Hagar outright cruelty. The relationship between Elizabeth and Mary could not be more different. With them there is no rivalry, no attempt to hurt, but greetings, a leaping for joy, blessing and song. If we search for biblical parallels, we might do better to look to the tale of Shiphrah and Puah, the two midwives in Exodus 1, of Moses' mother Jochebed and his sister Miriam (with the daughter of the pharaoh and her female slaves) in Exodus 2, or to the book of Ruth, and its tale of the love of two women, Ruth and Naomi. Yet while all these shine with courage, and speak of women cooperating together to work acts of unexpected salvation, none of them provides a close counterpart to Luke's story. In the Bible the meeting of Elizabeth and Mary stands alone.

In those days Mary went with haste to a Judean town in the hill country, where she entered the house of Zechariah

85

and greeted Elizabeth. When Elizabeth heard Mary's greeting, the child leaped in her womb. And Elizabeth was filled with the Holy Spirit and exclaimed with a loud cry, 'Blessed are you among women, and blessed is the fruit of your womb! Why has this happened to me, that the mother of my Lord should come to me? For behold, as soon as the sound of your greeting reached my ears, the child in my womb leaped for joy. And blessed is she who believed that there would be a fulfillment of what was spoken to her by the Lord.'         (Luke 1.39–45)

The writing is so sparse at the start of this passage. We only discover Mary is pregnant halfway through, when Elizabeth pronounces her blessing on 'the fruit of her womb'. Luke has refused to go into the circumstances of Mary's conception, or tell us who the father is. Now he omits to mention the timing of it. These things are of no concern to him. All that matters is the child she is now carrying.

Nor does Luke explain why Mary makes such a long journey, all the way from Galilee to the Judean hills, some 70 miles or more, to visit her relative. On the face of it, it is all highly implausible. She is still a betrothed woman, and as such would be expected to live in seclusion in her family's home. She is very young and, even if the usual customs were not adhered to, she could not hope to travel anywhere without her father or elder brothers accompanying her – she is still under their authority. And what is the purpose of her visit? We learned from Gabriel near the end of the annunciation scene that the two women are related, but that is surely not enough to explain Mary's journey, nor her hurry.

We can understand her more easily when we reach the story of Jesus' birth and the visit of the shepherds, who meet their own angel and go to Bethlehem in similar haste. Looking back from that scene to this, we can say that Mary cannot wait to see her relative, to rejoice with her over the news of her pregnancy, and to share the news of her own expected child and everything Gabriel has said to her. She may fear to break that news to her own mother, let alone her father, but she knows Elizabeth will understand. For Elizabeth is part of it all.

Gabriel has explained that. The stories of the two women are inextricably entwined together. By the terms of those stories it is, therefore, the most natural thing in the world that they should meet, that they should exchange greetings, that they should join together in celebrating what no one else yet understands, the bright purposes of God which underlie their pregnancies. It might seem at first that their situations are diametrically opposed to one another. For Elizabeth, her not conceiving a child was a source of shame and disgrace. Her pregnancy is a wonderful and marvellously unexpected end to that shame. Mary, however, is a betrothed woman, who must remain a virgin until her marriage to Joseph is completed. For her the conception of a child at this stage, however it is brought about, would seem to threaten disaster. But Elizabeth will understand what is going on and will find the divine thread that runs through it all. Gabriel has said so, or at least has spoken of Elizabeth in the same breath as he told of the empowerment and protection of God. Mary will find something of that empowerment and protection, if she goes to Elizabeth. No wonder she hurries! The story makes perfect sense! The actual implausibility of Mary's journey is neither here nor there, and thanks to Luke's supreme skill as a storyteller, we do not notice it, until some pesky writer points it out to us!

Mary's hopes are fully justified. She only has to utter her greeting and Elizabeth understands everything. The joy of the leaping child in Elizabeth's womb helps, of course. But so does Elizabeth being filled with the Spirit of God, and with the divine insight that brings.

One might think that the still embryonic John (as he will be called, once he is born) is somewhat precocious. But did not Gabriel tell his father that the child would be 'filled with the Holy Spirit even while he is in his mother's womb'? Some in Luke–Acts find themselves 'filled with rage' (Luke 4.28), with 'awe' (Luke 5.26), with 'mindless fury' (see Luke 6.11), with 'wonder and amazement' (Acts 3.10), with 'jealousy' (Acts 5.17; 13.45). Whatever it may be, they are taken over by it; it determines how they see things, how they feel, how they act; it is their driving force, their overriding energy. So to be 'filled with the Holy Spirit' is to be taken over by the energy of God, to see things through God's eyes, to share God's passion, to share God's creativity, to work God's work. When we reach Acts, we find Luke describing the followers of Jesus at the first Pentecost and a little later as 'filled with the Holy Spirit' (2.4; 4.31), and that same phrase is used of Peter in 4.8, and of Paul after his conversion (9.17; 13.9). Thus the phrase is used sparingly at key moments and of key figures. It is highly significant that in the Gospel it is first applied to an unborn child and a woman. Tables are being overturned here, and a hint is being given of just how radical Jesus' vision and practice will be, once he reaches adulthood. In the new 'family' he will establish, with God as the father, street children will be put centre stage, and women will find a new dignity and status. A new social order will be established. But it begins even before he is born! These two chapters of Luke are more than a prologue to the rest of his Gospel. The story of God's new work in Jesus starts here, with a pregnant old woman and the child in her womb, and, of course, with Mary also, who has herself been promised that the Holy Spirit will come upon her.

Luke will describe Jesus as 'full of the Holy Spirit', when he is about to embark upon his public ministry (4.1), and the scene that marks its beginning will describe him as coming in 'the power of the Spirit' (4.14), and will have him read from the scroll of Isaiah in the synagogue at Nazareth a passage that opens with the line, 'The Spirit of the Lord is upon me' (4.18; the Greek word for 'upon' is the same as that used by Gabriel of Mary). It is all of a pattern, God's pattern, and Elizabeth, the child she carries, and Mary are already weaving some of its fine intricacies.

The actual phrase 'filled with the Holy Spirit' occurs once more in Luke's Gospel, in 1.67, where its subject is Zechariah. But that is after John is born, when at last he finds the warm truth of the promise made by Gabriel in the sanctuary, and rediscovers his voice. For the moment Elizabeth puts him to some shame. We may think his punishment harsh, yet still, as Luke has written the story, it is Elizabeth who first finds the truth and the freedom to rejoice. Mary turns naturally to her, rather than Zechariah, and for the time being he is nowhere to be seen. It will be a similar story at the end of the Gospel, when Mary of Magdala, Joanna, Mary the mother of James and the other unnamed women with them will be the first to find the truth of the resurrection, and the male followers of Jesus will dismiss them as telling 'an idle tale' (Luke 24.1–11).

Elizabeth does Mary very great honour by the way she greets her. Mary is entering the house of an older relative. The etiquette of her times demands she give the first greeting, and so she does. But then, in calling her 'blessed among women' and 'the mother of my Lord', Elizabeth reverses those usual courtesies. She accords the higher status to her much younger relative, who is still only a girl and not even a fully married woman. It is yet another sign that with the coming of Jesus 'those who are last will be first, and those who are first will be last' (see Luke 13.30).

It serves another, more immediate purpose, to emphasize that Jesus will take precedence over John. Luke's Gospel, like the other three, is about Jesus. It concerns itself with John only in so far as he sheds light on the nature, significance and calling of Jesus himself. Despite the way this Gospel has begun, John will play a small part once Jesus is born. Beyond the birth narratives he has but one big scene, in 3.1–20, and curiously enough that will not include Jesus' baptism. Luke will hurry over that, and will not even say in so many words that John performed it (3.21–22). John also, born first, will end up last, or at least will take his place behind the figure of Jesus so as to be hidden from our sight.

So far, in this scene of the meeting of the two women, Elizabeth has done all the talking. Now Mary responds and in remarkable fashion. The two opening chapters of Luke's Gospel contain four songs. The first, Mary's Song, is the most famous of them all. Christians call it by the opening word of its Latin version, the 'Magnificat'. Like the other three, it is far from being a mere musical interlude. The songs give us a chance to reflect on the wider meaning of the surrounding narrative. Christians in this country have become less familiar with the Magnificat than they were. Even among regular churchgoers most now attend but one service a week, and be

that a Eucharist or Holy Communion, or else a time of infor-
mal worship built round contemporary songs and preaching
and prayer, Mary's Song will rarely if ever be included. But in
some places, such as the cathedral where I work, Evensong is
sung every day, and each time the choir sings the Magnificat.
In Joseph Fitzmyer's punchy translation, from the first volume
of his Anchor Bible commentary on Luke (1979), with two
alterations ('humiliation' for 'lowliness'; 'slave' for 'handmaid'), it goes like this:

> And Mary said,
> 'My soul declares the greatness of the Lord,
> and my spirit finds delight in God my saviour,
> because he has had regard for the humiliation of his
>    slave.
> From now on all generations will count me blessed,
> for he who is mighty has done great things for me,
> he whose name is holy.
> His mercy is for those who fear him from generation
>    to generation.
> He has displayed the might of his arm;
> he has put to rout the arrogant in the conceit of their
>    hearts.
> He has put down mighty rulers from their thrones and
>    exalted the lowly.
> He has filled the hungry with good things and sent the
>    rich away empty.
> He has come to the aid of his servant Israel,
> mindful of his mercy,
> as he promised our fathers, Abraham and his
>    descendants forever.

> (1.46–55)

One might say this is not a distinctively Christian poem.
Whether it was composed by Luke himself or not (some would
say he is quoting a song written by another Jewish Christian,
which was already being sung in Christian communities), it
draws its language and its theology from the Jewish Scriptures.
As Joel Green puts it in his New International Commentary
(1997, p. 101), it is 'a virtual collage of biblical texts'. Though

full of phrases drawn from the Psalms, it takes its main inspiration from the Song of Hannah in 1 Samuel 2.

Hannah sings her song to celebrate the birth of her son Samuel. It includes lines such as these:

> My heart exults in the Lord . . .
> I rejoice in my deliverance.
> The bows of the mighty are broken,
> while the feeble gird on strength.
> The sated have hired themselves out for bread,
> While the hungry are fat with spoil.
> It is the Lord who makes poor and makes rich,
> who brings low, and yes, exalts!
> He raises the poor from the dust,
> he lifts the needy from the dung heap,
> to give them a place among princes,
> and grant them the seat of honour.
> (1 Samuel 2.1a,d, 4–5a, 7–8a, my own translation)

The echoes of such lines as these in Luke's poem are unmistakable. We have the same God who turns things on their heads and reverses people's fortunes, and who wields a mighty arm as a victorious warrior-king. And each of the two songs moves from the particular to the general, from the situation of the woman who sings it, out onto a wide stage, placing her experience among the wonders God has done for his people and the promises he has given them. In each case a child is being celebrated, one new-born, the other still awaiting birth, who will usher in a new era for that people and give rise to a new expectation that their fortunes will be reversed. The songs speak to a people who are longing for freedom from oppression, from the grip of the Philistines and a corrupt priesthood in the one case, from the Romans in the other. Though neither is a call to revolution, they are both triumphant in tone.

We would not wish either to get into the wrong hands. Their danger lies in their use of the ancient image of God as warrior-king. The theologies of the ancient Near East were forged in the palaces of kings and by the servants of kings. What more natural that they should dress God in the fine robes or the armour of a king? And what more tragic? In our own times we are still suffering grievously from the use of such language, and we have not rid ourselves yet of this macho god who struts his stuff all over the place, or calls upon his followers to do his dirty work for him. It remains a weakness of Mary's Song that it has not entirely shaken itself free of such things, and we fail to notice that only because, in our mind's ear, we have given the singer such a meek, submissive voice. Hannah's is the song of a feisty woman. So, in truth, is Mary's.

Is there another similarity between the two songs? 1 Samuel 1 explores the hurt Hannah endures at the hands of Peninnah. Both are the wives of a man called Elkanah, and their story is the old one of the loved, but barren wife (Hannah), and the unloved, at least the less loved, but fertile wife (Peninnah), and their inevitable rivalry. That same chapter brings Hannah to the shrine at Shiloh and into contact with a priest called Eli, who mistakes her praying for drunkenness and tells her to stop making a spectacle of herself. When Hannah sings her song in chapter 2, she is gloating over the imminent fall of her enemies. In my book *Sarah Laughed* I wrote:

> Hannah raises her head high above the rival who once taunted her, and the high priest who took her for a drunkard. She pokes her musical tongue out at them, and will have them for breakfast . . . She rejoices that Peninnah's child-bearing days are over, or soon will be, and that Eli will soon be toppled from his prestigious position, and will no longer be able to treat the worshippers at Shiloh with such disdain.      (p. 135)

Does Mary's song touch upon *her* hurt, and celebrate the victory God has given her over her own enemy? The answer to that will much depend on how we translate the Greek word *tapeinosis* in its third line. A common translation is 'lowliness', and that in turn has been understood as either humility or a reference to Mary's humble origins. The emphasis on Mary's humility, common among many Christians, depends a good deal on interpreting her response to Gabriel as a meek subservience. But I have already argued against such a reading of the text. Humble origins Mary certainly has, however, and Luke has gently drawn our attention to them by first locating Gabriel in the magnificence of the Jerusalem temple, and then moving him to Mary's house in Nazareth. Yet Fitzmyer, despite his translation 'lowliness', admits the usual meaning of *tapeinosis* is 'humiliation', and that is certainly the case in the Greek Septuagint version of the story of Hannah in 1 Samuel 1. Three times there we hear of how Peninnah continually taunts Hannah because she cannot have children, and the story-teller goes out of his way to emphasize how much hurt this causes. Hannah turns to heartfelt prayer. The prayer begins like this: 'She was deeply distressed and prayed to the LORD, and wept bitterly. She made this vow: "O LORD of hosts, if only you will have regard, have regard for the *tapeinosis* of your slave . . ." ' (1 Samuel 1.10–11a). This chapter in 1 Samuel says nothing of Hannah's lowly origins. If anything, the reverse is the case. But of her humiliation at the hands of Peninnah the story speaks loudly. It is plain that verse 11a should be translated 'if only you will have regard for the *humiliation* of your slave'. Now Mary's line, 'because he has had regard for the *tapeinosis* of his slave', is lifted almost word for word from Hannah's prayer. I see no need to translate *tapeinosis* one way in 1 Samuel 1.11, and another in Luke 1.48. Jane Schaberg discusses the translation 'humiliation' at some length in her book *The Illegitimacy of Jesus*, pp. 97–101, and in Mary's case finds there a veiled reference to the experience of rape. Many will be outraged by such a suggestion, but we have already seen that Luke's annunciation story, and Gabriel's refusal to answer Mary's question about how she would conceive, have left that experience as a terrible possibility. If Schaberg is right, if, at least, hers is a possible reading of the text, and surely it is, then the verse in Mary's song about God putting to rout 'the arrogant in the conceit of their hearts' takes on a new and startling meaning, and even the next one and its declaration that God 'has put down mighty rulers from their thrones and exalted the lowly' comes to have another reference.

One thing more we can add, however. Hannah's abuse is audible not only in her prayer but in her song, and we can catch there something of the damage it has done to her. There is a grating edge to some of the lines, a certain vindictiveness. In Mary's case, there is a purer celebration, the song of a woman who has risen high above any hurt that might have been done to her, the song of a girl, who though she has some new theology yet to learn from her son, has indeed been touched by the Spirit of God.

# 11

## A priest finds his voice and sings

━━━◆◆━━━

Luke's story continues with this:

> And Mary remained with her about three months, and
> then returned to her home. Now the time came for
> Elizabeth to give birth, and she bore a son. Her neigh-
> bours and relatives heard that the Lord had shown his
> great mercy to her, and they rejoiced with her.
>
> (1.56–58)

When Gabriel appeared to Mary, Elizabeth was already six
months into her pregnancy. It now seems as though Mary
herself must have conceived her own child in the weeks
immediately following that encounter. It was a common view
in the ancient world that pregnancy lasted ten lunar months
(see Wisdom 7.1–2). If we allow some three to four weeks for
Mary to become pregnant and travel down to Judea, and add
the three months she stays there, then she must leave just
before Elizabeth comes to full term.

Why does she leave just at the crucial moment? Could she
not stay a few more days, perhaps one more day, and join in
the celebrations? The answer lies with the art of biblical storytelling and Luke's in particular. There may be a crowd on the
edges of the stage, but a biblical scene tends to have but one,
two or three main characters in the centre. Luke himself likes
to clear his decks before he begins a new scene, and to make
sure the spotlights fall on its chief characters, and that others
do not provide any distractions. For him the scene of John's
birth and circumcision belongs to but three figures: Elizabeth,
Zechariah and John himself. He cannot risk Mary stealing the
limelight. She must return home. We hear nothing about what
happens when she gets there, and we never will.

Elizabeth brings her son safely to birth and the rejoicing begins. Gabriel promised Zechariah there would be a party (1.14). But the neighbours and relatives do not know the half of it yet. All they know is that at last, beyond all hoping, Elizabeth has a child, a son, and that is excuse enough. Indeed it is, but they are about to learn there is more to this son of hers than they realize.

> On the eighth day they came to circumcise the child and they were going to name him Zechariah after his father. But his mother said, 'No; he is to be called John.' They said to her, 'None of your relatives has this name.' Then they began motioning to his father to find what he wanted the child to be called. He asked for a writing tablet and wrote, 'His name is John.' And all of them were amazed. Immediately his mouth was opened and his tongue freed, and he began to speak, praising God. Fear came over all their neighbours, and all these things were talked about throughout the entire hill country of Judea. All who heard them pondered them and said, 'What then will this child become?' For indeed the hand of the Lord was with him. (1.59–66)

What are the neighbours and relatives doing, wanting to name the child? Some of them, no doubt, have been present at the birth itself. It was usual for women of neighbouring households to provide help when a woman went into labour, and to join in the celebrations when a child was safely born. At the end of the story of Ruth 'the women of the neighbourhood' are there for the birth of Ruth's son, and begin the party afterwards. They do also give him his name, Obed (Ruth 4.14–17). Do the neighbours of Elizabeth and her relatives assume they have a similar prerogative? Yet the story of the naming of Obed is highly unusual. There is no other case in the Bible where the neighbours name a child. Normally it is the mother (28 times in the Hebrew Scriptures), or the father (18 times). And their suggestion that Elizabeth's son should be called after his father is also unexpected. The practice may be relatively common in the contemporary United States and elsewhere but, as far as we know, it was not so in first-century

Palestine. We seem to have a storyteller's device here. Their wanting the baby to be called Zechariah reminds us how little they as yet understand. *We* know what is going on, for we have overheard what Gabriel said to Zechariah in the sanctuary. But they were not there, of course. Luke has let us into the secret and put us in a superior position. It is the kind of thing biblical storytellers often do and, if truth be told, it is one of the sources of the delight we find in reading their material. In this particular case the neighbours' seeming interference performs another function, neatly preparing the way for the little miracle with the writing tablet and Zechariah's recovering his hearing and his voice.

They start signing to Zechariah. We did not realize that he has been deaf as well, but in those times muteness was often associated with deafness. It means he has not heard Elizabeth saying the child must be named John. It does indicate, however, that he has managed to convey to her what happened in the sanctuary and what the angel said. That makes him a better husband than Abraham! In Genesis 17 God spends almost the whole chapter speaking with Abraham, and gives him the momentous news that he and his wife Sarah will have a son. Yet in the next chapter, when God turns up in disguise in the heat of the afternoon, Sarah has to learn the news for herself by overhearing the conversation between God and her husband while she is taking a break from the washing-up! She has been waiting not years but decades for a child, has been driven to distraction by her childlessness; yet, when finally, and against all expectation, the glad tidings are given, her husband does not bother to pass them on to her! Thank God, Zechariah is more sensitive than Abraham, and his marriage a stronger one. Elizabeth knows exactly what her baby should be called, and no doubt she understands exactly why.

There are two things the neighbours and relatives for their part cannot understand: how Zechariah chooses the same name as his wife for their child, and how and why suddenly he can hear and speak again. Again we know the answers. And we can see that the period of Zechariah's punishment for his bewilderment is over. He is, after all, a man who is 'righteous before God, living according to all the commandments and ordinances of the Lord, blameless.' The difficulty he found in believing the angel's promise has rendered him deaf and dumb and removed him from the story for a spell. But now he is back. And now he can hear. And now he can speak. And now he can sing.

Then his father Zechariah was filled with the Holy Spirit and spoke this prophecy:

> 'Blessed be the Lord, the God of Israel,
> for he has looked down upon his people and has
>     redeemed them;
> he has raised up for us a horn of salvation
> in the house of his servant David,
> as he spoke through the mouth of his holy prophets
>     from of old,
> that we would be saved from our enemies
> and from the hand of those who hate us.
> Thus he has shown the mercy promised to our
>     ancestors,
> and has remembered his holy covenant,
> the oath he swore to our ancestor Abraham,
> to grant us that we, being rescued from the hand of
>     our enemies,
> might serve him without fear,
> in holiness and righteousness before him all our days.
>
> And you, little child, will be called the prophet of
>     the Most High,
> for you will go before the Lord to prepare his ways,
> to give knowledge to his people of salvation in the
>     forgiveness of their sins.
> Through the merciful compassion of our God,
> the dawn from on high will look down upon us,
> to give light to those who sit in darkness and in the
>     shadow of death,
> to guide our feet into the way of peace.'
>
> (1.67–79)

It is not insignificant that Luke chooses poetry to reflect on the meaning of the events his narrative describes. Poetry of this kind has a solemnity about it; it is significant speech, which can penetrate further into truth than prose. Sometimes only poetry will do. Or music. Luke has given us both, for again he has given us a song to sing. Still in our cathedral we sing it, or the choir does, at services of choral Mattins. It is called, again by the first word of its Latin version, the Benedictus.

Like Mary's Song, like all the songs in these two chapters of Luke, it is a very Jewish piece. 'Scriptural echoes [are] present in practically every clause,' says Joel Green in his commentary (p. 112). It would be perfectly at home embedded in some Old Testament narrative. As in the case of Mary's Song, it is its context that gives it another dimension and makes it Christian.

If Luke has not composed it himself, but taken or adapted it from a song being sung in the Christian communities he knew, then he has chosen it with care. For this is not just any Jewish song; this is a priest's song, or at least gathers to itself a special energy when it is given to a priest such as Zechariah to sing. When he emerged from the sanctuary of the temple, was he not supposed to bless the people by reciting the words from Numbers 6, 'The LORD bless you and keep you; the LORD make his face to shine upon you, and be gracious to you; the LORD lift up his countenance upon you, and give you peace'? His song begins as a benediction rather than a blessing, but still it echoes the tone, language and theology of those verses in Numbers. Zechariah also tells of the mercy of God, and compares it to the light of the sun; he too speaks of the compassion of God for his people and his protection of them; like the Numbers blessing, his song ends with the word 'peace'.

Zechariah's Song is one for those in the dark, or those who live in the shadow of death. Its background is oppression, or the fear of it. As a priest, Zechariah rejoices that now his people will be able to 'serve' their God without fear. In that word 'serve' he is thinking of the worship of the temple, where ten months ago he found more holiness than he had bargained for. Less than 200 years earlier a Greek Emperor, Antiochus Epiphanes IV, who called himself a god and had himself portrayed on his coins looking like the Greek god

Zeus, had erected an altar to Zeus in the Jerusalem temple over the altar of burnt offering. The temple was rededicated to Zeus. The Jews had managed to reclaim it, but then the threat came from Rome. When Zechariah comes out of the sanctuary and tries in vain to pronounce the blessing of the people crowding round its entrance, we have to imagine them being looked down upon by Roman soldiers. For by this time Roman troops were stationed in the Antonia Fortress, at the northwest corner of the temple courts. One day those soldiers will make sure that when Jesus causes mayhem in the temple, he does not get away with it.

In our own day many worship their God in fear, or under the thumb of those who threaten and continually humiliate. By a tragic irony, the Christians of Bethlehem and East Jerusalem are among them. For them Zechariah's Song will have a special poignancy.

There is a strong nationalism to Zechariah's Song. But it lacks the militant tone of some of the verses of Mary's Song. The age-old image of God the warrior-king still lies beneath some of its lines, but it is more muted, especially in the second half, which Zechariah addresses to his son. I imagine him singing these lines holding John in his arms. To take any newborn child or grandchild into our arms is to hold a great mystery. The miracle of birth has the knack of putting us in touch with heaven. The infant John puts Zechariah in touch with the salvation God brings, with his forgiveness, his mercy and warm compassion, his light, his hope and truth, and his peace. In Isaiah 40 we find a most beautiful poem composed in the darkness of exile in Babylonia, that speaks of God's homecoming. It is read in churches in Advent, as we wait to tell once more the Christmas story.

> A voice cries out:
> 'In the wilderness prepare the way of the LORD,
> make straight in the desert a highway for our God.
> Every valley shall be lifted up,
> and every mountain and hill be made low;
> the uneven ground shall become level,
> and the rough places a plain.

Then the glory of the LORD shall be revealed,
And all people shall see it together.'
                                        (Isaiah 40.3–5a)

This prophet/poet dreams of a great ceremonial highway
being built across the trackless desert from Babylon to
Jerusalem, with God leading his people home like a shepherd,
carrying the 'lambs' in his arms and taking special care of the
'nursing ewes'. Luke will quote from the poem, the same lines
as we have, when he comes to speak of the preaching of John
and his work of baptizing the people (3.4–6). Meanwhile,
Zechariah tells his tiny son that 'he will go before the Lord to
prepare his ways'.

But who does he mean by 'the Lord'? God, of course. Jesus,
of course. It is time for Jesus to be born, and that is Luke's
judgement also. He concludes Zechariah's Song with one brief
note about John: 'The child grew and became strong in spirit,
and he was in the wilderness until the day he appeared publicly
to Israel' (1.80).

With that he clears the stage once more. We are ready to
go to Bethlehem.

# 12

## Entertaining God unawares

The Letter to the Hebrews has the famous verse: 'Do not neglect to show hospitality to strangers, for by doing that some have entertained angels unawares' (see 13.2). The writer must have had Genesis 18.1–15 at the top of his mind when he wrote that. But he gets it wrong. For Genesis 18, one of the most brilliantly written pieces in the Bible, and one we have already had cause to mention, is a story about entertaining God.

It concerns Abraham and begins like this:

> And the Lord appeared to him in the Terebinths of Mamre when he was sitting by the tent flap in the heat of the day. And he raised his eyes and saw, and look, three men were standing before him.
>
> (Genesis 18.1–2, Robert Alter's translation)

The Hebrew verb behind 'appeared' in verse 1 and 'saw' in verse 2 is the same. That underlines what the opening phrase makes plain enough, that it is God himself, admittedly accompanied by two heavenly companions, who stands in front of the snoozing Abraham. Everett Fox makes that explicit in his own somewhat less elegant, but more literal translation of the Hebrew: 'Now [the Lord] was seen by him by the oaks of Mamre . . . He lifted up his eyes and saw' (*The Five Books of Moses*, 1995, p. 75). The trouble is that Abraham is having a siesta when God appears, and when 'he peers out through the shimmering heat waves of the desert noon' (Robert Alter again, in a footnote to his translation of this passage: *The Five Books of Moses*, Harvill Press, 1995, p. 85, note 1), he thinks he sees three human travellers. As the passage proceeds, he never does realize who the strangers are.

But he does spring up from where he is sitting to become a model of hospitality (though still far from a model husband!):

> He ran toward them from the tent flap and bowed to the ground. And he said, 'My lord, if I have found favour in your eyes, please do not go on past your servant. Let a little water be fetched and bathe your feet and stretch out under the tree, and let me fetch a morsel of bread, and refresh yourselves. Then you may go, for have you not come by your servant?' And they said, 'Do as you have spoken.' And Abraham hurried to the tent to Sarah and he said, 'Hurry! Knead three *seahs* of choice semolina flour and make loaves.' And to the herd Abraham ran and fetched a tender and goodly calf and gave it to the lad, who hurried to prepare it. And he fetched curds and milk and the calf that had been prepared and he set these before them, he standing over them under the tree, and they ate.                   (18.3–9, Alter's translation)

Abraham does not know what he is doing. All he knows is that three strangers have come to his tent in the heat of the day, and he must offer them shade, water for their feet and food and drink. Let us be clear. It could be a matter of life and death. The strangers are on foot in the desert and it is very hot. If Abraham lets them go on their way without entertaining them, they might die, at least if they are the human beings he takes them for. True, the meal he and Sarah and the lad prepare is vast, but even that is not so very unusual. Abraham must maintain his honour and his status. By providing such a huge meal he demonstrates to his visitors that he can afford it. By honouring them he gathers honour to himself. Of course, he makes light of it – 'let a little water be fetched . . . a morsel of bread' – but that is all part of the courtesy.

Such hospitality is still to be found in many parts of the world and in many communities. My family and I have experienced it for ourselves in Russia. It is always to be found in Sikh gurdwaras, as again I know well. Someone I met once at a conference told me of the time 50 years ago when he was a young merchant seaman, 16 years old, and had come off a

# The Christmas Stories

ship in Cardiff docks. He was walking through the streets trying to find the railway station. A Muslim man was sitting outside his house, and he stopped to ask him the way. 'I can give you directions', he told him, 'but when is your train due to leave?' When he learned it was not for another two hours, he took him inside his house and gave him a lavish meal. He had never met that man again, but 50 years later the memory of his generosity had not faded.

I heard another story recently of an English couple's visit to Basra in Iraq, not long before the outbreak of the first Iraq war. Exploring one of the mansions beside one of the city's canals that had once belonged to a Jewish merchant, they came upon an Iraqi woman with her children. The house was in such a state they had not realized a family was living there. They seemed to have virtually nothing, but at once the woman made them welcome, pulled up some of the floorboards, lit a fire, and baked them some cakes. She and her children stood by as they ate.

Why do I relate these stories of hospitality before we set off for Bethlehem? If we pay close heed to Luke's story, the answer will eventually become clear.

> Now it happened in those days a decree went out from Caesar Augustus that all the world should be registered. This registration was the first and it took place when Quirinius was governor of Syria. All went to be registered, each to their own town. So Joseph also went up from Galilee, from the town of Nazareth, to Judea, to the city of David, called Bethlehem, because he was descended from the house and family of David. He went to be registered with Mary, to whom he was betrothed and who was pregnant. While they were there, the time came for her to give birth, and she gave birth to her firstborn son, wrapped him tight in bands of cloth, and laid him in a manger, because there was no room for them in the guest room.　(Luke 2.1–7)

Again the scene that Luke paints is not an entirely plausible one. In Matthew's story, as we have seen, Bethlehem is Mary's and Joseph's home village, and there is no need for them to

104

go anywhere for the birth. Jesus is born at home, Joseph's home, for by the time the child arrives, he has completed the marriage and taken Mary to live with him. Luke, however, not only says that Mary and Joseph come from Nazareth, but has Mary come to full term during the period of betrothal. Would she, could she, really make the long journey to Bethlehem with Joseph, when she is still living with her parents and under their authority?

The setting of the registration that Luke has provided does not fit with historical fact, either. John Dominic Crossan makes the difficulties plain:

> [It] seems a brilliant explanation of why Jesus of Nazareth was born at Bethlehem unless, of course, one knows anything of Roman history and Roman . . . bureaucracy. First, there never was a worldwide census under Augustus. Second, the Palestinian census was undertaken by the Syrian legate, P. Sulpicius Quirinius, in 6 to 7 CE, about a decade after the birth of Jesus . . . Third . . . the Roman custom was to count you in the place of your domicile or work and not in that of your ancestry or birth . . . to record people in their ancestral rather than their occupational locations would have constituted a bureaucratic nightmare.        (*The Historical Jesus*, 1991, p. 372)

Once more, however, for the purposes of the story, its artistry and its power, such implausibility and inaccuracy matter not one jot or tittle. Whether Luke understood exactly what John Crossan understands, we shall never know. But we can be sure that as an artist, as a storyteller, he knew precisely what he was doing.

By putting Jesus' birth against the background of Augustus and a worldwide census he at once gives the event a worldwide significance, and pitches the kingdom of God against the empire of Rome. When Gabriel appears in the temple to speak of the coming birth of John the Baptist, it is 'in the days of Herod king of Judea'. By that introduction Luke suggests that John's significance will be chiefly for his own people. Jesus, however, will be a man for the whole world, and that world will never be the same once he is born. That is why it is

Augustus, not Herod, who now is mentioned, and why we hear of a registration of 'all the world'. In the second volume of his great work Luke will tell how the news of Jesus spreads far beyond Judea and Palestine, and how communities of his followers are established in city after city of the Roman Empire. He ends his story with Paul, the founder of so many of those churches, at the centre of the empire, preaching and teaching in Rome itself.

Luke does not go into detail about what kind of emperor Augustus is. He would have known very well that he came to be worshipped as a god, and during his lifetime allowed himself to be called 'Son of God'. He would have known that one of his titles was 'Saviour', and that he was hailed as the one who had brought peace to 'all the world'. Paullus Fabius Maximus, proconsul of Asia (the western part of modern Turkey), proposed that the beginning of the year should be moved to Augustus' birthday, the birthday of the one he called 'the most divine Caesar'. He declared, 'We could justly hold it to be equivalent to the beginning of all things . . . and he has given a different aspect to the whole world, which blindly would have embraced its own destruction if Caesar had not been born for the common benefit of all.' In the last year of his life the emperor was sailing in the gulf of Puteoli, when he was hailed by the crew and passengers of a ship that had come from Alexandria. The writer Suetonius describes the scene: 'Clad in white, crowned with garlands and burning incense, [they] lavished upon him good wishes and the highest praises, saying that it was through him they lived, through him they sailed the seas, and through him they enjoyed their liberty and their fortunes.'

But what does Augustus mean on the ground, in Palestine, among those who have no say in anything and no authority of their own? Luke's story provides us with one small but telling example. Augustus can click his finger in Rome and send a young man on a journey of at least 85 miles to get his name on the precious imperial list. And the girl to whom that same young man is betrothed has to leave the proper seclusion of her family home and travel with him. She is pregnant with her first child. Does the rest of her family travel with her? Presumably not, since it is Joseph's family who come from Bethlehem, not hers. The other members of her family are probably heading in another direction, or else staying in Nazareth. In that case, she leaves behind her mother, her older sisters if she has any, and the women among their neighbours who would normally help her during her labour. How do she and Joseph travel? Paintings, films and carols have invariably given them a donkey to sit on, Mary, at least. But there is no donkey in Luke's story. How far is Mary into her pregnancy? She stayed three months with Elizabeth, and might have been three or four weeks pregnant by the time she arrived. She had to travel back to Nazareth afterwards. Her time will come after they reach Bethlehem. How long it is between their arrival in the village and the birth Luke does not say, but judging by what he has told us, we have to think of Mary travelling, probably walking, while heavily pregnant. Will she give birth on the way? Will there be anyone to help? Will her child be born in a ditch? Will she survive the ordeal? Will her child live? These are not overly dramatic questions to ask. If we pay heed to what Luke tells us and use our imaginations, we will not be able to stop ourselves asking them. Luke does not talk of Mary's fear and anxiety, nor of Joseph's, but we can unearth them from beneath the surface of his text. So much for the 'most divine Caesar' and his saving the world from destruction 'for the common benefit of all'!

Yet once Mary and Joseph reach their destination, things are not nearly so bad as the nativity plays and all the rest have so often given us to understand. In the opening chapter of this book I retold Pat Alexander's story of Wallace Purling, the boy who played the innkeeper in a nativity play at his school in the USA, and who was moved enough by Mary and Joseph's pleading to offer them his own room. Those of us with children or grandchildren are used to nativity plays where Joseph and Mary do not just knock on one door, but several, and each time are turned away. In the end they have to take shelter in a stable, among the animals. Painters of the scene have often made it even worse, turning this stable into a ruin, and writers of prayers, wishing to emphasize Jesus' association with the poor, have called it 'dirty' or 'filthy'. Yet where is the stable in Luke's story? Nowhere. And where is the 'inn'? Well, we do find one in many translations, and still in some scholarly commentaries. But those translations and commentaries are probably wrong. As Joel Green points out in his commentary (pp. 128–9), Bethlehem was only a small place and, not being on any major roads, probably had no inn. The Greek word so often translated 'inn', *kataluma*, occurs in one other passage in Luke's Gospel, as Green also points out, in the story of the Last Supper, in 22.11. There it is generally translated 'guest room'. In the Parable of the Good Samaritan, when the Samaritan takes the man he has rescued to an 'inn', he takes him not to a *kataluma*, but to a *pandocheion* (Luke 10.34).

Yet the strongest argument for there being no inn in this story comes from its cultural background. We have seen already, and in this very passage, how much Luke leaves to the imagination. But what will the first hearers of his Gospel, listening to this particular story being read in their Christian communities late in the first century, themselves imagine? What scene will they picture in their mind's eye at the point where Mary and Joseph arrive in Bethlehem? 'Why,' they will tell us, 'Joseph's relatives take them in, of course! How could we think anything else?'

The rules of hospitality are clear. Luke's story, told later in his Gospel, in 10.1–12, of Jesus sending out 70 of his followers into the towns and villages of the countryside is illuminating. The passage demonstrates that strangers can conceivably be turned away, but also that they can reasonably hope for board and lodging from people they do not know at all, and with whom they have no prior connection. In such a society, family members are surely never turned away, or only where there has been a serious family feud. Bethlehem is where Joseph's family comes from, and we know of no quarrel among them. Almost certainly there will be relatives of his, distant perhaps, but related nonetheless, still living there. They will look after him, and Mary, too, and when her time comes, the women of the family will help, and the neighbours as well, and if there is a midwife in the village, she will be sent for. If perchance no relatives are left, then some family will take them in. The villagers will certainly not leave them out on the streets, particularly with Mary in her condition. They will bring great shame upon the whole village if they do, and Bethlehem will never live it down. In any case, they will quickly perceive that it is not just a matter of hospitality, but of life and death. There is no maternity hospital up the road. If they do not help, Mary and her child might well die. 'Enough babies and mothers giving birth do', they will say, 'even when they are indoors with all the help that can be mustered. And it gets cold in Bethlehem at night.'

If we wish to get into the world of Luke's story, we would do well to recall those stories of hospitality with which this chapter began.

At least there is a manger, and Jesus is laid in one. But we are talking of houses, like those still existing in many parts of the world, and which were found not so many years ago in the UK, where the family's animals are kept at night under the same roof. So the manger is not in a stable at the back, but inside the house, and Jesus is laid in that simply because there is not enough space for them all in the guest room. Where exactly the birth takes place, Luke does not quite say. Is it in the guest room, and then later Mary and Joseph put the baby to sleep in the manger for safety's sake? After all, the house will be small, and there is a family already living there, and the guest room is hardly that, really, but only a curtained-off area, and it is very cramped and not the best place for a baby, and there may well be more senior relatives in the house who have also come to Bethlehem for the registration. Is that it? Is that what Luke's hearers will imagine? Or will they, despite all we have suggested about their hospitality, smell something of a snub?

Their rules of hospitality demand that any service offered should be of the very best kind. Think of the story of Abraham and Sarah in Genesis 18. Think of the contemporary Palestinians, still famous for their hospitality, despite all their difficulties. Or think of St Petersburg in Russia. When a family put up my wife and me and our four children in their small flat in the city, they vacated the place in the evening, after insisting on doing all the washing-up, went and slept in some relative's flat down the road, and then crept back in the morning to make breakfast. They did not think they were doing anything extraordinary. Now some suggest Luke introduces the detail of the manger to catch an echo of Isaiah 1.3, where God is heard to say, 'The ox knows its owner, and the donkey its master's manger; but Israel does not know me, my people do not understand me.' The question remains, however: whether or not they make any connection with Isaiah, what will Luke's hearers think about the manger, particularly the women among them? It is, perhaps, a strange place to put a newborn child. That seems clear from the story of the shepherds, which follows immediately after this one. So will they say, 'In the circumstances it's the best place for the child. An unusual idea, sure, but a very sensible one.' Or will they mutter and say, 'The family should have made more effort and found something better'? It is hard to say. If Mary and Joseph are being snubbed here, then we can perhaps guess why, and hear the family themselves whispering to one another, 'They're still only betrothed! They should have waited to have a child till after the marriage was completed. We'll take them in, of course, and look after the girl, but we won't get out the best china.'

Whatever we suppose, the family has no idea what is really going on. No doubt they will presume the child is Joseph's. But more than that, much more, they will have no idea of the meaning of the child born under their roof. Abraham once entertained God unawares, or so the story goes. Are they, in their own understandable ignorance, doing the same? We might say so, and some shepherds will certainly soon make them think.

Meanwhile, the teachers who plan their nativity plays had better choose some children for some new parts. They will not need to find an innkeeper, but they will need a family and the women from the neighbouring houses, and perhaps a midwife. The animals can stay, of course.

# 13

## *Shepherds*

———◆◆◆———

In both Matthew and Luke, Mary, Joseph and Jesus receive some unexpected visitors: in Matthew's case magi, in Luke's shepherds.

Now there were shepherds in the region living out of doors, keeping night watch over their flock. An angel of the Lord stood before them and the glory of the Lord shone around them, and they were terrified. But the angel said to them, 'Do not be afraid. For behold, I am bringing you good news of great joy, news for all the people: to you is born this day in the city of David a Saviour, who is the Messiah, the Lord. And this will be a sign for you: you will find a child wrapped in bands of cloth and lying in a manger.' And suddenly there was with the angel a multitude of the heavenly host, praising God and saying,

'Glory to God in highest heaven,
and on earth peace among those upon whom his
    favour falls!'

If we are not careful, this story will not hold any surprises for us any more. It will be too familiar, and we will be too used to half-listening to it being read in carol services, or singing the famous carol and thinking of the old joke about shepherds washing their socks by night. When I taught biblical studies in a theological college, before we entered a particular passage, I used to ask the students to try to hear it or read it as if for the first time. So let us pretend we have never heard this story before. Let us try to catch some of its surprise.

For it is, I believe, more surprising than the story of the magi. Magi were known to predict the fall and rise of kings. They could walk corridors of power, as we have seen. They watched the heavens, and could see what others missed. But shepherds! What is special about shepherds? (If you are reading this and are a shepherd yourself, or married to one, or the child or grandchild of one, please forgive my question.) True, Jesus has come to birth in Bethlehem, David's village (Luke calls it David's 'city'), and when we first hear about David in the Hebrew Bible, he is watching over the family flock (1 Samuel 16.11). 'Shepherd', too, was an ancient royal title, and appears in that guise in the Hebrew Bible, most famously perhaps in Ezekiel 34. But these 'shepherds', living out in the open, are hardly kings in disguise.

Nor are they from Bethlehem, it seems. Luke's description of them is very interesting. The word he uses of them suggests they do not just happen to be in the open air that particular night. It is their home. They are not from another village. They are not from any village. Later in the Gospel (15.4–6), Luke will tell Jesus' Parable of the Lost Sheep. It speaks of 100 sheep. That is a large flock, and Luke's hearers, and Jesus' before him, will have imagined them being in the care of several shepherds, although the little story only puts the spotlight on one. When a sheep goes missing, that shepherd goes in search of it, leaving the other 99 in the wilderness. We have to picture the other shepherds then taking those 99 back to the village pens for the night, for when the lost sheep is found, that is precisely what its shepherd does with it. He carries it home, and gets the whole village together for a party. The shepherds in Luke 2, however, live out in the open all the time. That is why they are out there with their flocks during the night, taking it in turns to watch for any wolves, lions or bears that might be around. They are nomads. Today we would call them Bedouin.

Commentators on this passage used to emphasize how much religious Jews despised shepherds in those days, thinking them dishonest and as having no heed for the demands of the torah. But there is no hint of such prejudice in the Parable of the Lost Sheep, nor in John's reflection on Jesus as 'the good shepherd' (John 10.1–18). The only figure who does come in for blame in that reflection is the hired hand, who does not own the sheep, nor care for them, and runs away when a wolf comes. Shepherds who look after their own animals come in for high praise, for John says they are prepared to lose their lives for them: 'The good shepherd lays down his life for the sheep' (10.11).

There is no suggestion in Luke 2 that the shepherds who come to Bethlehem are hired hands. Being nomads, they will be looking after their own sheep. Nor for that matter does Luke dwell on their 'goodness'. He does not relate how they have just risked their lives fighting off a pack of wolves just before the angel appears. But they *are* outsiders. Nomads always are. In today's Israel–Palestine they are, and their own plight in the current troubles is hardly ever mentioned in our media, though there are plenty of tales that could be told. They are literally and metaphorically 'out there', out of sight, out of hearing, out of mind, beyond the edges of civilized society, or so 'civilized society' still sometimes likes to think.

In having nomadic shepherds the first to learn the truth about the infant Jesus, Luke is making a highly significant claim about the workings of God and about the kind of figure Jesus is and soon will be. This new 'king', this new Messiah, or Anointed One, could not be more different from the 'divine' Augustus! Indeed, he turns all notions of kingship and of the exercise of sovereignty on their heads. Imagine the first people to greet a new Roman emperor being a bunch of nomadic shepherds! This Messiah will not gather about him a great horde of flunkies and sycophants. His kingdom will be, as John Crossan has put it, a kingdom of nobodies. No one will make clearer than Luke in his Gospel how Jesus draws about him the despised, the forgotten, the 'little people', those who normally have no say in anything, those who are on the edge, out of sight, out of hearing, out of mind. The Jesus of his Gospel comes as very good news indeed to those who most need to hear some. He puts at the front of the queue those who are used to being at the back. And he brings them into the heart of the love and mercy of God, and tells them they are members of God's family, his very own children.

That nomadic shepherds should be the first to come to Bethlehem is both utterly astonishing, and entirely appropriate; indeed, just what we might have expected!

Heaven has moved in these stories further and further from the acknowledged centres of power. The angel first appeared in the Jerusalem temple, then to Mary in tiny Nazareth, buried in the Galilee hills. Now he comes in the dark of night to a place with no name, beyond the fields cultivated by the farmers of Bethlehem, beyond the lights and chatter of houses, to where the only sounds are the crackling of a fire, the shuffling of sheep, the snoring of a few men, and the singing of the stars. Though Luke will take us back to Jerusalem in the next scene, and to the temple also, his Gospel will lead us eventually to a death on a cross, where Jesus will in one sense be as far from the human centres of power as anyone can be, and where the love and mercy of God are yet finally revealed in their full majesty.

The way Luke describes the encounter with the angels is familiar to us by now, with fear and awe being met with the ringing words, 'Do not be afraid.' The angel tells of who Jesus is: he is the Messiah, the one his people have been waiting for as the years and centuries have rolled by. And he is 'Saviour' and 'Lord'. Augustus has those two titles, also. But Augustus' day is over. A new emperor has emerged, to establish the empire of God, and 'If you wish to see what kind of empire that is', the angel tells the shepherds, 'go and find a baby wrapped in bands of cloth, lying in an animal feeding trough. Stand round that manger and you will know. This very day God has come out of hiding. You will find yourselves looking level-eyed into the face of God.' A veritable throng of angels then sings the third of the four songs of these birth stories, joining heaven and earth together, and binding them with chords of praise of God and peace. That peace is offered to all, for with the coming of Jesus all humankind is enfolded in the mercy and favour of God.

The shepherds are told they will find the child in the 'city of David'. The angel is playing with them, just as Luke was playing with us, when he spoke in the previous scene of Joseph 'going up' 'from Galilee, from the town of Nazareth, to Judea, to the city of David'. Such a description would normally mean Jerusalem. For Jerusalem is 'the city of David', and Jews in Palestine would naturally have talked of 'going up' to it, just as people in England speak of 'going up' to London. But then, in case we made the same mistake as the magi, Luke put us right: 'to the city of David . . . called Bethlehem'! Bethlehem was not a city, of course. John calls it what it was, 'the village where David lived' (7.42). Luke's description is playful. But the shepherds do not need any help. At once they understand what the angel means.

> When the angels had departed from them into heaven, the shepherds said to one another, 'Quick! Let us go to Bethlehem and see this thing that has taken place, which the Lord has made known to us.' So they went with haste, and found Mary and Joseph and the child lying in a manger. Seeing it all, they made known what had been told them about the child. All who heard them were amazed at what the shepherds told them. But Mary treasured all these things and pondered them in her heart. The shepherds returned, glorifying and praising God for all they had heard and seen. It was just as they had been told it would be. (2.15–20)

The shepherds leave for Bethlehem in a state of great excitement, and without any hesitation. When the magi visit the child Jesus, they do, of course, have much further to travel, but they go at first to the wrong place. And though they stir up 'all Jerusalem' and greatly interest Herod, they take the Bethlehem road on their own. The people of Jerusalem do not accompany them, or run ahead of them, and Herod bides his time, waiting for more intelligence about the street and the precise house where he should send his soldiers. The shepherds, however, cannot wait. The angels have overwhelmed them. They recognize at once that angels are only God in disguise, and that it is God who has shared his secret with them, made things known that no others know. And when they get to the place, they are not disappointed. They find what some painters of the scene have managed to capture: all heaven in a small baby lying in the straw. And they discover the beginnings of a new order, where women come before men: they find not Joseph and Mary, but 'Mary and Joseph'. The change in the usual order will not have been lost on Luke's first hearers and readers.

The shepherds bring no gifts with them. That is not necessary. What is required of them is that they should do God's work, and so they do, 'making known' what he has 'made known' to them. Mary and Elizabeth have rejoiced together, and Zechariah has sung his song to a wondering audience. Yet these nomadic shepherds become in Luke the first to celebrate and proclaim the meaning of the birth of Jesus. They return 'praising God', just as the angels were 'praising God' in their song. They are Jesus' first disciples, although Jesus himself cannot yet understand what they are saying, or even focus his eyes upon them.

For her part Mary, still recovering from the birth, cannot quite take it all in. But she holds it deep in her heart, until the time when all will be clear. The last time we hear of Mary in Luke's great work, she is among the followers of her son. She is praying with them, waiting for a great outpouring of God's Spirit that he has promised. Like the others she has met him risen out of death, and witnessed his ascension (Acts 1.14). All is plain then, and she can at last understand why the shepherds were so excited.

# 14

## *Back in the temple*

Luke ends his stories of the birth of Jesus where he began, in Jerusalem, in the temple. He will not take us inside the sanctuary this time, for there is no priest in these final episodes. Nor will there be any need for Gabriel. This time heaven will come to God's temple held in a mother's arms.

When first we heard of Zechariah and Elizabeth, Luke told us they were 'righteous before God, living according to all the commandments and ordinances of the Lord, blameless'. Mary and Joseph are presented in the same way. They circumcise the child on the eighth day, as the Torah required (Leviticus 12.3); they call their child Jesus, just as Gabriel told Mary they should; they go up to Jerusalem for Mary's purification after childbirth and make the necessary offering, again in accordance with the Torah (Leviticus 12.2–8); and they bring their firstborn son to the temple, thus fulfilling the requirement of Exodus 13.2. For the first time in these two long chapters, which are so full of echoes of the Jewish Scriptures, Luke actually quotes the text, a few words from Exodus 13 first, then a phrase from Leviticus 12. He wishes to make quite clear how meticulous Mary and Joseph are in their obedience to the Torah. They are exemplary Jews, just as Zechariah was, despite his initial bewilderment, and Elizabeth, too. In the precincts of the temple, we will meet two more.

> When eight days had passed, it was time to circumcise the child, and they named him Jesus, the name given by the angel before he was conceived in the womb.
>
> And when the time came for their purification according to the law of Moses, they brought him to Jerusalem, to present him to the Lord (as it is written in the law of

the Lord, 'Every firstborn male shall be called holy to the Lord'), and they offered a sacrifice according to what is prescribed in the law of the Lord, 'a pair of turtledoves or two young pigeons'.

Now there was a man in Jerusalem whose name was Simeon. This man was righteous and devout; he lived in expectation of the consolation of Israel, and the Holy Spirit was upon him. It had been revealed to him by the Holy Spirit that he would not see death before he had seen the Lord's Messiah. Guided by the Spirit he came into the temple, and when the parents brought the child Jesus, to do for him what was customary under the law, Simeon took him in his arms and praised God saying,

> 'Master, now you are dismissing your slave in peace, according to your word;
> for my eyes have seen your salvation,
> which you have prepared in the presence of all peoples,
> a light for revelation to the Gentiles
> and for glory to your people Israel.'

The child's father and mother were amazed at what was being said about him. Then Simeon blessed them and said to his mother Mary, 'This child is destined for the fall and the rise of many in Israel, and to be a sign that will be rejected so that the thoughts of many hearts will be revealed – and as for you, a sword will pierce your soul, also.'

There was also a prophet, Anna, the daughter of Phanuel, of the tribe of Asher. She was of a very great age, having lived with her husband seven years after her marriage, and then as a widow for 84 years. She did not leave the temple, but worshipped there night and day with fasting and prayer. At that moment she came up, and began to thank God and to speak about the child to all who were living in expectation of the deliverance of Jerusalem. (2.21–38)

We have already found reminiscences of the story of Hannah and the birth of Samuel in these stories: like Hannah, Elizabeth endures years of childlessness, and then has a son of great significance for her people; Mary sings her great song, her Magnificat, basing it on Hannah's own song in 1 Samuel 2, telling of her humiliation and her triumph, as Hannah does; before that, in the presence of Gabriel, Mary declares herself 'the slave of God', picking up the way Hannah describes herself. There are two further significant links with Hannah in this present passage. Near the end of it a woman appears who shares Hannah's name – 'Anna' is the Greek version of the Hebrew 'Hannah'. And the whole scene, with its concern with the presentation of Jesus to God, reminds us that when Hannah prays to God, she vows that if a son is born to her, she will give him back to him, or lend him to him for the whole of his life (1 Samuel 1.11, 28).

Yet there are differences, also, between the two stories. Simeon and Anna are very different from Eli, the priest of the sanctuary at Shiloh who sees Hannah praying, and with whom she speaks when she returns with her son, to lend him to God. Eli's sons are guilty of greed, corruption, sexual abuse of women, and blasphemy. Yet Eli turns a blind eye to all but the sexual abuse, and pays more attention to what he takes for drunkenness in Hannah, when she first prays in her distress for a child. 'How long are you going to stay drunk?' he asks her. 'Shake off the effects of your wine!' (see 1 Samuel 1.14, my translation) Admittedly, he does eventually give Hannah his blessing. Discovering from her that she is praying, though without knowing what she is praying for, he sends her on her way with the words: 'Go in peace; the God of Israel grant the petition you have made to him' (1.17). When Hannah's child is born, however, and grows up a little, the first task God gives him is to announce to Eli the destruction of his family.

Not for the first time Luke has taken a tale crossed with dark shadows and filled it with light. He heaps praise on both Simeon and Anna. In contrast with Eli and his sons, they represent the very best within Judaism, both of Palestine and the diaspora.

In a detailed discussion of Anna in his book *Gospel Women* (2002), Richard Bauckham suggests she represents the northern tribes, who were exiled from Palestine in the time of the Assyrians, late in the eighth century BC (*Gospel Women*, pp. 98–9). Luke is careful to tell us, he points out, that she comes from the tribe of Asher, and Luke is not in the habit of including such details just for the sake of it. The tribe of Asher originally had their territory in the western hills of Galilee, and that region was, as the archaeologists tell us, completely stripped of its population by the Assyrians. Those who were not killed were deported. So Anna is the exemplary ambassador of the Jews of the diaspora, come to Jerusalem to fast and to pray for the city's deliverance and for the return of her people to that holy centre of the world, and to the temple at its heart. In the small Jesus she recognizes the moment, the figure, she has been waiting for all those many years. Her fasting days are over!

Bauckham believes it perfectly possible that Anna was an historical character. Such a devout woman, always in the temple, and living to such a great age, would certainly, as he says, have become well known in Jerusalem, and would have been talked about for a long time. 'There is nothing improbable in the idea,' he says, 'that she appeared in traditions that reached Luke, directly or indirectly, from the Jerusalem church' (*Gospel Women*, p. 99). That remains so, even though we may concede that the age Luke or his tradition gives her, 105, owes more to an attempt to divide her life into neat periods of seven years: 14 years before her marriage, seven as a married woman, 12 times seven as a widow.

If Bauckham is right, then it is a particular shame that Luke does not give Anna a song to sing, like that of the original Hannah, or like Simeon's. We hear of Anna thanking God, but we do not hear her words. She too should have a song to sing. Simeon, who Bauckham regards as a native of Jerusalem, tells in his song of the salvation and the light of God spreading out from the city and its temple to all the scattered tribes of Israel, and to the world of the Gentiles. He is right to celebrate, of course. The whole book of Acts will be devoted to that theme. Yet Luke's narrative, in both his Gospel and in

Acts, will also keep drawing us back to Jerusalem, and at the great scene of Pentecost, near the beginning of Acts, Jews from all over the world will be gathered there for the feast and will hear about 'God's deeds of power' performed through Jesus (Acts 2.5–11). That Pentecost will mark the beginning of the Church, and Anna's dreams will find some grand fruition. Women are so prominent in these two opening chapters of Luke's Gospel, and in the scene we are examining much more attention is still given to Mary than to Joseph. And when the Bible as a whole takes hardly any notice of the spiritual life of women, we can certainly compliment Luke on the care he takes to explain Anna's. It is just a pity that there is not a more exact balance in his narrative, and that we are not given a chance to hear either Anna's speaking or her singing voice.

Though still the light of God shines brightly in this scene, there is one shadow cast over it by Simeon. 'This child', he tells Mary, 'is destined for the fall and rise of many in Israel, and to be a sign that will be rejected – and, as for you, a sword will pierce your soul.' When Jesus is grown to manhood, and begins to teach and heal in the villages and towns of Galilee, then 'some are last who will be first, and some are first who will be last' (Luke 13.30). The 'first' will not be best pleased. Many of them will turn away from the truth that is in front of their eyes, and will be so threatened by it, they will try to destroy it. They will put the man who embodies it on a cross, and teach him to die. Then another righteous Jew, another man who is 'living in expectation of the kingdom of God', Joseph of Arimathea, will take down his body and give it burial. Mary will play no part in that story. She does not appear at the crucifixion in Luke. Only John puts her at the foot of the cross. We will not hear her name mentioned again until that scene near the beginning of Acts, when the followers of Jesus are praying together and waiting for the incoming wave of the Spirit to crash over them. Yet Luke, in a few words of Simeon, gives encouragement to those many painters who portray the sadness of Mary as she holds her infant son, a mother contemplating the future that awaits her child and the pain she will bear. 'A sword will pierce your soul.'

Luke is warning us here, too, as Simeon is warning Mary. These two chapters of his have featured only the righteous: Zechariah, Elizabeth, Simeon, Anna, Mary herself, Joseph, the shepherds. Though Augustus can throw his weight about, and leave the likes of Mary and Joseph to bear the consequences, he is still far away in Rome, and is not planning to send any soldiers marching for slaughter into Bethlehem, or Jerusalem, or Nazareth. Things will not be always like that. 'As for you, a sword will pierce your soul.'

Something of the pain that awaits Mary is, in fact, revealed in the very next scene, the one that brings the stories of the birth of Jesus to a close. Strictly speaking, it is not about the birth, since Jesus is now 12 years old, but Luke ties it in with the scenes that precede it, and it is the preaching of John the Baptist which follows it in chapter 3 that begins the new act in his play.

Now every year his parents went up to Jerusalem for the festival of the Passover. And when he was 12 years old, they went up as usual for the festival. They completed the days of its observance, but when his parents started for home, the boy Jesus stayed behind in Jerusalem. His parents did not realize. Assuming he was in the group of travellers, they went a day's journey. Then they began looking for him among their relatives and friends. When they did not find him, they returned to Jerusalem to look for him. After three days they found him in the temple, sitting in the middle of the teachers, listening to them and asking them questions. All who heard him were amazed at his understanding and his answers. When his parents saw him, they were utterly astonished, and his mother said to him, 'Child, why have you treated us like this? Look, your father and I have been terribly worried searching for you.' He said to them, 'Why were you searching for me? Did you not know that I must be in my Father's house?' But they did not understand what he meant.

Then he went down with them and came to Nazareth, and was obedient to them. His mother treasured all these things in her heart.

And Jesus advanced in wisdom and in years, and in divine and human favour.                    (2.41–52)

We must not think of this as describing the occasion of Jesus' *bar-mitzvah*. We cannot be at all certain that Jews observed such a ceremony in Jesus' day. Nor must we assume this is the first time he has travelled with his parents to Jerusalem for the Passover. Luke has gone out of his way to stress what a devout family they are, and so encourages us to imagine they have been coming every year. But this is the first time we have heard Jesus open his mouth, and his words provide the crux of the passage.

There were similar stories about Moses and Samuel being theologically precocious. Exodus tells us nothing about Moses' boyhood, but Josephus, the first-century Jewish historian, knows stories about it, and informs us that the 'understanding' (the same word as Luke uses in 2.47) of the three-year-old Moses was far in advance of his years. The boy Samuel grew up 'both in stature and in favour with the LORD and with the people' (1 Samuel 2.26) a verse that is clearly brought to mind by the final line of Luke's passage, and then 1 Samuel 3 contains the famous story of God calling to the young Samuel in the night. The stories of Samuel have already played a major role in the way Luke has composed his own birth narratives, and have been one of their chief sources of inspiration. It is, therefore, especially interesting to hear Josephus reporting the legend that, 'Having completed his twelfth year, Samuel was already holding the office of prophet.'

Yet the words Jesus says to his mother are more significant than his wowing the teachers and theologians in the temple. 'Did you not know that I must be in my Father's house?' Already he is calling God his 'Father'. Perhaps we understand a little better now why Joseph plays such a small part in these narratives, and in this scene also. Simeon addressed Mary in the last scene and said nothing specifically to Joseph, and in this last passage Mary does all the talking for the two of them. It is through Joseph, the man who adopts Jesus as his child, that Jesus can trace his descent from David. Joseph is needed so that Jesus can be called Messiah. Apart from that, he has almost no role to play. It is *God's* being Father that will be so significant for Jesus, and for his followers, also. When Jesus comes to form his new family, they will all count as children of their Father God, and their belonging to that family will override their ties of blood. So, though Jesus returns to Nazareth with Mary and Joseph and remains for the time being under their authority, he has already made clear where his true allegiance lies. Already he is preparing them for the time when Mary and his brothers will stand outside his circle, wanting to see him, and he will say to those around him, 'My mother and my brothers are those who hear the word of God and do it' (Luke 8.21).

Meanwhile, we are told, 'Mary treasured all these things in her heart.' Luke invites us to do the same. All along he has presented Mary as a model disciple, and he would have us keep her company. Why else would he have composed these extraordinary stories for us to hear, to enjoy and to consider?

# 15

## Further reflections

Our little collection of reflections in Chapter 7 related to Advent and to Matthew's stories of the birth of Jesus. The ones I offer now take Luke's narratives as their starting point. The first is a fairly straightforward meditation on his story of the annunciation to Mary and its biblical background. In the other three I have made free use of my imagination and introduced details not found in Luke at all. The fourth is particularly notable for the freedom with which it plays with the biblical text, but I hope to good effect. My playing with the Bible is never casual nor, I hope, presumptuous. After all, these pieces were all composed for preaching in the context of Christian worship, and my overriding concern was to reach out for the mystery of God and to help the congregation touch it for themselves.

'Annunciation' and 'The shepherds' have already been published, the first in *Keeping God Company*, the second in *God Treads Softly Here*. 'In the dark of the world's turning' and 'An old man waiting' appear here for the first time.

### Annunciation

*There is a play on words in this piece, which needs some explanation. Our earlier chapter on Luke's story of the annunciation, in its translation of the passage, had Gabriel greet Mary with the words, 'Rejoice, most favoured one!' The root of the Greek word behind 'favoured' is* charis, *a term which is common in the New Testament and is often translated 'grace'. So in my meditation, recalling the Church's common description of Mary as 'full of grace', I have taken the liberty of having Gabriel, or rather the God who comes in the guise of Gabriel, call her 'the graced one'.*

In times far distant,
almost beyond our horizon,
and out of Luke's reach, also,
so it would seem,
God himself appeared
for annunciation.

He came himself to Hagar's desert,
by the well at Beer-lahai-roi.
Hagar saw God,
saw *God*,
and named him, too!
God left Hagar's well
proudly bearing a new identity,
a new name,
her name for him,
her mark upon him,
for ever and ever, Amen.

God came himself,
wrapped in awe,
to the wife of Manoah,
to tell of the birth of her son,
slipped into the house
when Manoah was not looking,
met her a second time,
most outrageously,
out in the open,
when again Manoah was off the scene!

By the time we reach Luke's story,
God has long ceased walking the earth, it seems.
Cut off in heaven,
he must send an angel,
trailing his divinity.

Yet Mary is as amazed as Hagar was,
as unnerved as Eluma,
rabbi-named wife of Manoah.
Gabriel has his own name, for sure,
in all the paintings his own wings also,

and private disc of light about his head.
Yet surely 'Gabriel' is another name for God.
Surely Hagar and Eluma both tell us that.

So God himself comes to Nazareth,
unseen, unheeded by all
except this young woman.

She is not ready for him,
she is not ready for a child, either.
She is only betrothed,
not yet married.
A child too soon will spell ruin,
for her, for Joseph,
for their families.
If she is pregnant now,
her young form will swell with disgrace,
and bring forth disaster.
She cannot contemplate a child.
Not yet.

And yet
this Gabriel-God comes to speak
of pregnancy, of birth,
of a son, of naming,
of greatness, thrones and kingdoms,
and all the while
can tell of nothing but grace!
He calls her
'the graced one',
graced, engraced, all-graced.
He tells her
she has found grace already;
he has sheltered her,
will surely shelter her
beneath the wide wings of his divinity.
They will be enough to hide her from contempt.

More than that,
much more,
the wings of God

will be the coverings of her palanquin.
'The Holy Spirit will come upon you,
and the power of the Most High will overshadow you.'
This is coronation talk!
Language fit from ancient times
for a king,
new-minted for a queen.
Disgrace is turned quite all to grace!
Her son
(her son!)
will be the son of God!
She will ride in his entourage!
'Here I am,' she says,
'the Lord's slave,'
meaning no humiliation,
but honour, and power,
and fine reflected glory.
For Moses also,
of shining face,
was 'the slave of God',
and Abraham, Isaac, Jacob, too,
Joshua, David, the prophets,
and a woman who came so close to annunciation,
the mother of Samuel, the king-maker,
Hannah.
'Here I am, the Lord's slave.'
These words put Mary in fine company!

The empire of distant Rome
in which she lives
is run by an emperor's slaves.
She counts herself in much higher company!
She is too good for Augustus!
She walks *God*'s corridors of power;
shares *God*'s secrets.
She is God's confidante,
the bearer of his child!
For her son,
the son that spelled such ruin,

will be the Son of God,
grace, engraced, beyond grace.

Give her a note,
and this young woman
will sing a queen's song,
that we will call 'Magnificat'!

And when she is done,
and her voice has died away,
then we must listen for the rustle of God's wings,
see their shadow enfolding us,
feel again the warmth,
the eternal safety
beneath their shelter,
smell the sweet scent of God's grace,
and taste and see
in a disc of bread and a sip of wine
how good,
how very good,
the Lord is.

For here too,
as once in Nazareth,
as always in God's company,
disgrace is turned quite all to grace.


## In the dark of the world's turning

*As becomes clear in its second half, this piece was composed for a Christmas Day. I preached it in Chester Cathedral in 2005.*

In the dark of the world's turning
a small light shines.
No flash of an explosion;
none is shaken out of bed,
or terrified out of their wits;
no glare turned into the face,
to make one shield one's eyes
and tremble at the questioning to come;
no beam sent searching the black sky

for enemies, to find them and destroy;
nothing remarkable at all, you might think,
until you see the angels all a-dance.

The good people of Bethlehem and the bad
sleep on undisturbed,
and wake the next day
believing nothing has changed.
Only one family in one small house
has had a sleepless night.
For they could not let a girl
have her child on the street
or in the cold of a ditch.
They embraced her and her young man
with the warmth of Bethlehem hospitality,
gave her room for the birth,
sent for the neighbours to help.

There was hardly room for them all
in the stumbling dark of the night:
women from the houses next door,
the women of the family,
the grandmother who had seen it all before so many
     times,
the mother who had four of her own,
and the eldest of her daughters,
fetching and carrying,
and standing on tiptoe trying to see,
frightened for this Mary
whom they had never seen before,
who was so young,
so far from home and the women she knew –
no mother to attend her –
so bewildered by it all,
as if she was taken by surprise,
while the waves of pain crashed upon her
and she did not know whether her child
would ever turn towards birth,
or would die shut up inside her,
and she herself would not survive,

but find a shallow grave
so far from Nazareth.

Yet in the dark of the world's turning
the light does shine,
and the narrow streets of Bethlehem
are filled with sheep and goats
led by shepherds
come to warm their hands around the fire of God.
They too have had a sleepless night,
kept awake by angels
who stole their pipes,
brought in drums and trumpets,
turned their quiet fields to carnival,
told them they could not rest
till they had been to Bethlehem and seen for themselves.
So they have bent their heads into the house as well,
followed by their animals
to join the ox and ass,
while the women of the family
have brought them food and drink
and they have greeted a young man
they have never seen before,
who says his name is Joseph
and cannot keep the smile off his face.
They stand eating and drinking,
looking into the manger,
seeing for themselves
what the angels said they must see,
knowing they will never be the same again.

And in the dark turning of our world,
that same small light shines
to make us glad
and know we will not be the same again.

Do not mistake,
that child was not born
to drag us screaming into merriment.
We are told by so many at this dark time of year
we must be happy,

as if cheerfulness is compulsory,
until the bright festivities are over
and the usual routines are resumed.
Yet that is hard, crushing hard to bear,
if death and grief have come too close;
if the consultant has confirmed too many of our fears;
if love has gone cold;
if we are bullied or abused;
if drugs or booze have had their bitter way,
if debt has risen to the roof;
if this Christmas, like the rest, we are alone.

But did you know
one of the shepherds had just lost his wife,
and the mother of the house where the child was born
had buried three of her own stillborn,
the last just days before?
They needed more than most to see that child
lying so small, so alive in the hay,
to find the miracle of it all,
to sense the warmth of it coursing through their veins,
to know they touched the very Truth of God.

The ground had rocked beneath their feet,
cracked open, leaving them reeling on the edge.
Beside that manger they stood on the world's bedrock,
unshakable.
They had not known which way to turn,
but when the child was born they found the gate to
   God's garden.
They had wondered whether anything mattered any more,
but then felt God's gentle, strong embrace,
wrapped round to keep them from the cold.

And they knew this child
was not for them alone,
although they held him close.
The truth of this child's birth,
the pain of it,
the fear of it,
the relief of it,

was the world's meaning
and the world's peace.
Nothing else could compare.
They knew that in that house,
no different from the rest,
God himself had come to birth.

And as they gazed upon him lying in the hay,
the old idols came crashing down.
No more the god enthroned in distant splendour,
surrounded by his sycophants;
No more the god who clicked his finger
to decide between life and death;
no more the god who rode into battle,
to leave the ground strewn with the bodies
of those who dared contest his power;
no more the god who shovelled the dead
into the monster's mouth of hell,
lest the comfort of his heaven be disturbed.

The God who had come to birth in Bethlehem
had no power at all,
except the power of love.

And what great power that was, that is!
It fills the hearts of those who look upon him,
it fills the house,
flows through the streets towards Jerusalem,
surrounds its grand temple,
spreads north to Galilee
and far, far beyond,
to reach a city strangely quiet
and a cathedral that has been waiting four weeks for it
    to arrive.

So now it is our turn
to offer God our hospitality.

## The shepherds

*1st shepherd*   I tell you, we didn't know what we would
find at the end of our journey. We thought
we knew. We had our expectations.

133

| | |
|---|---|
| *2nd shepherd* | It was not as we thought it would be, and we will never be the same again. |
| *3rd shepherd* | We are shepherds, illiterate, of course, Bedouin, not Jews, nor Romans, nor anyone that counts; semi-nomadic, living the other side of the fence of what you call civilization. We were the last people you would expect to lead you to the mystery of God. |
| *2nd shepherd* | That is why we went on our own. |
| *1st shepherd* | Not from the fields below Bethlehem. We came out of the desert, as we always do, knowing we would find God at the end of our journey, but expecting the wrong one. |
| *3rd shepherd* | The God we knew lived among us in the desert, searching with us for lost sheep, carrying lambs in his strong arms, playing midwife to the ibex and the antelope, untying the ropes of the stars to let them pasture in the fields of the night, tilting the waterskins of heaven to make it rain and covering the hills with flowers, soaring with the eagle, turning in the sun with the migrating storks, treading through the silence, and dancing uproariously to our pipes. Our women sometimes came across her at the well, and knew her always at times of birth and death. |
| *2nd shepherd* | Yet we expected to find the god the clever people spoke of, the god who lived at the end of long corridors of power, where we would never be allowed, or could feel at home if we were, the royal god for whom, you might say, gifts of gold, frankincense and myrrh were appropriate. |
| *1st shepherd* | We had no such gifts to bring, of course. Quite out of our league. |
| *3rd shepherd* | You might ask why we went at all, if we didn't expect to be allowed near him. Why set out for an inaccessible god, when we had God so close to us in the desert? |

| | |
|---|---|
| *1st shepherd* | We wished to find answers to some old, nagging questions: Had we made our God too parochial? Had we confined our God to the desert and its ways? Was our God of our own making? Was our God too small? |
| *2nd shepherd* | We thought for a moment he was, when we came in sight of Jerusalem and saw its temple. We had given our God a tent, to mark his presence with us. Not to live in, of course. Our God stretched far beyond the stars, was larger than the desert's silence, deeper than its sand and rock. But we had given him a tent as a mark of our hospitality, to make him feel he belonged, to shelter him against the cold of the night and the heat of the sun. |
| *3rd shepherd* | The temple in Jerusalem was not made of goat skins, as our tent was. Had we forgotten the grandeur of God? At first the temple made us think we had. Should we have learned to be afraid of God? The temple made us wonder. |
| *1st shepherd* | It made us mighty uncomfortable, too. It lacked generosity. Its god lacked generosity. Our God was free, and had given us the freedom of the desert. This temple-god was surrounded by rules and regulations, the rules of the city, the regulations of powerful men, who used them to lord it over the likes of us. |
| *3rd shepherd* | Our women could not imagine meeting that god at the well. |
| *2nd shepherd* | So we were relieved when we realized the temple did not mark the end of our journey. We were drawn on, to an out-of-the-way place, to a side street, to a one-roomed house with an animal stall under its roof and a feeding trough on its floor, to a family – the one whose house it was – |

standing there, grandmother, mother with a baby in her arms, father, six other children, and a young girl exhausted from the pain and terror of giving birth, her man kneeling beside the feeding trough, and a newborn baby, tight wrapped, lying in the straw.

*1st shepherd*  We felt at home in that place, more at home than we had ever felt before. We were most welcome.

*3rd shepherd*  They gave us food and drink, of course, the family of the house. Later the entire village came together and put on a feast to mark our coming and the birth of the child. They killed their fatted calf. We sat in a single circle under the stars and ate together, men, women and children. We had never seen anything quite like it before.

*2nd shepherd*  When the child woke up and had been fed and winded, his mother let us hold him, each one of us in turn.

*3rd shepherd*  I can still feel that small weight. It contained all the love of heaven and all earth's hope and longing! Have you ever held God in your arms?

*1st shepherd*  He *was* the God we knew so well, but closer still than we had ever dreamed. Against our cheeks he was! We had feared we had made our God too small. Truth is we had not made him small enough. He was not as we expected. But then, God never is.

*3rd shepherd*  What would happen when he grew to a man, we wondered, and saw that temple in Jerusalem?

*2nd shepherd*  I still carry God in my arms. When I go down to the wadi with the sheep and the goats, I still carry God in my arms.

*3rd shepherd*  When I climb to the top of that ancient holy mountain I know so well, I carry God in my

|            | arms, also, to show him the beauty of his world. We listen together to its silence. |
|------------|-------------------------------------------------------------------------------------|
| *1st shepherd* | When the soldiers come to humiliate us and keep us waiting in the sun, or ransack our tents, terrify our children and rape our women, I still carry God in my arms and hold him very tight, and find that he is holding me. |
| *2nd shepherd* | And when we sit all of us round the fire under the stars, in one single circle, men, women and children together, and eat and drink and tell our tales and play our pipes and lutes and sing and watch the small children dance and catch them when they fall, we still hold God in our arms and bounce him on our knees. |
| *1st, 2nd, 3rd shepherds* | Here, you hold him for a moment. |

## An old man waiting

An old man waiting.
Waiting for his heart's desire,
waiting for his God to move,
to speak those ancient words again,
'Let my people go!'
waiting for him to clear the land of occupation,
waiting for Rome to be put in its place,
waiting for the time
when they will not hurt or destroy
on all his holy mountain,
and the earth will be full of the knowledge of God
as the waters cover the sea.
An old man waiting for justice, for peace,
for the consolation, the contentment of his people,
waiting for the knowledge that all is well,
that no longer will the fetid air sound
to the beat of the helicopter
and the crying beyond all bearing of the mothers and
  their children,

nor the smooth-paved street to the wail of the ambulance
rushing to yet more pools of blood
and bodies twitching in the grasp of death.
An old man waiting for his heart's desire,
while the soldiers look down through the smoke of
    sacrifice
upon the courts of the house of God,
to make sure they are kept in good order
and nothing gets out of hand.

An old man waiting.
He has been so for a long time,
waiting for his God to emerge from his hiding
behind that heavy curtain,
to shake off the dust of holiness,
to walk out into the world and see.

He has been waiting all his life for the Messiah,
has this old man Simeon,
like the rest of us,
waiting for a Messiah,
waiting for hope to win the day,
waiting for God to do something,
waiting for a song to sing.

He has been waiting all his life
and this very morning
he has opened up his breaking heart
for God to overhear:
    'You told me, when my hair was black
    and my knees both worked,
        that I would not die before your fine Messiah came
    and hope was born anew.
    Well, my God, I wish you to know
    that the time now left to me is short –
    I can sense it in my bones.
    I have been waiting all these years,
    through famine, pest and plague,
    through settlement and wall of fear
    and buses blown to bits,

and here I am, my God,
but not for many weeks or days.
Must I die a hopeless death,
knowing that you do not keep your word?
My eyes are failing fast, my God,
so sooner than I care to say
I will not see him,
if the Messiah comes.
After all this time I will not *see*!
You have disappointed me too long, my God.
Do yourself proud before I die!
Let him come, your Messiah,
let him come and bring you from your hiding place!
Let me die with hope
knowing it is not all a lie.
Let me sing my song before it is too late,
the music dried up in my throat.'

The curtain bends aside,
enough for a girl from Nazareth
to emerge carrying a child in her arms.
She should have known better, of course.
What was she doing, for God's sake,
in the Holy of Holies?
Feeding him with the milk of her breast?
She slips across the court,
head bent down towards her child,
to leave this temple and its self-importance
for the hills of Galilee,
for a place where she will not be noticed,
and her child can play.
She is almost out of the temple now,
when she sees an old man waiting,
and knows full well,
in an instant,
in the twinkling of an eye,
that he is waiting for her,
or rather for her child.
He has waited all his life for this moment,

for her, Mary of Nazareth,
and her small child,
held against the beating of her heart.
How can she refuse him?

So now,
this very moment,
this most holy time,
she stands before him,
waiting for him to notice them.

His eyes are shut against the light;
he cannot look into the sun.
The breeze stirs Mary's skirts,
but he does not catch the movement.
She says nothing,
and he cannot hear the fall of her breath.
And so she adds her waiting to his.

And then the child cries,
and the old man opens his eyes and sees.
'You can sing your song now, old man,'
the young girl says.
'Sing him a lullaby
and calm his fear.
There is too much of it here.'

The old man has not been waiting all this time
for such a small Messiah.
But slowly, fighting the pain in his knees,
he stands, straightens, stretches out his arms
to receive the child.
'Oh Mary!'
is all he finds to say.
She smiles at him,
not asking how he knows her name.
Yet still, in his enfolding arms,
the child cries with fear.
'Sing him now your lullaby,'
the young girl says.
'Let him ride home

on the back of your song,
to where we will be safe.
Sing now, old man,
you have been silent for too long.'

So Simeon sings his song,
sings of light and peace,
salvation and glory,
while the young girl turns her skirts
and dances before him,
dark eyes flashing,
bare feet curling, slowly, gently spinning.
To her quiet rhythms
the old man rocks the child,
and all for that time is holy,

and an old woman's fasting days are done!
Anna, exiled Anna,
has come home to Jerusalem,
hoping for her God.
This day,
this hour,
this song,
this dance
she is not disappointed.
For more years than she can tell,
she has been bent towards the ground,
and never could she sing, even as a girl.
But now, but now
she joins Mary in her rocking dance,
faster, faster,
till they are stamping out their glee
and with the rest of their breath
adding women's voices to the old man's song,
while the child sleeps against his cheek.
Such a day! Such a day!

And still, and still the dance goes on.
Their song is never finished,
nor will ever end its Gloria.

# 16

## *The God who lies in a manger*

━━━◆◆◆━━━

Our explorations of the stories of the birth of Jesus in
Matthew and Luke have thrown up some conclusions which
would surprise many Christians, and many outside the
Church who have heard 'what Christians believe'.

Matthew shows no interest in Mary's spiritual life. In his
stories Mary remains in the shadows. He does not give us a
chance to speak of her faith or her righteousness. God in
Matthew 1–2 communicates with Joseph and with the magi,
but not with Mary. Like the God we find in the vast majority
of the pages of the Bible, he does not know how to speak to
women. At least, that is how he is made to seem. We cannot
even praise Matthew's Mary for her obedience. Again typical
of the women in the Bible, she simply does what her husband
tells her. Indeed, Matthew is so uninterested in Mary for herself that we do not hear at any point of Joseph doing the
telling. We have no dialogue between them, or even mono-
logues where Joseph explains what is going on. At the bidding
of heaven, he decides what they must do, and they do it. Mary
is entirely under his authority, and that is never questioned.

Luke is quite different. Now it is Joseph who is out of the
spotlight, and Luke 1–2 is highly unusual among biblical texts
for the attention it pays to the relationship between God and
women, not just Mary, but Elizabeth and Anna, also. All three
are presented as exemplary characters, women who have
touched the hem of God's garment or, rather, been caught up
in its folds. And yet we do not find in Luke the deferential,
submissive Mary that so many have painted, whether on
canvas or in their preaching or teaching. Obedient, yes.
Submissive, no. She does not bow her head, but holds it up
high. There is a defiance, a claiming of dignity and status in

her calling herself 'God's slave', and in the song she sings in Elizabeth's company. She is not the good little woman that men in the Church have so often made her out to be.

Nor does Matthew or Luke make clear how Jesus was conceived. They have little time for the question. Mark, John and Paul have no time for it at all. In Luke, Gabriel sidesteps Mary's question about how she will become pregnant, and the matter is not raised after that, though Mary in her song sings of how God has heeded her 'humiliation' and replaced it with honour. In Matthew the famous quotation of Isaiah 7.14, 'Behold, the virgin shall conceive and bear a son', cannot bear the huge weight of doctrine that is so often piled upon it. It is far too ambiguous for that, and its ambiguity does not rest on whether we translate the Greek word *parthenos* 'virgin' or 'young woman'. That is neither here nor there. As we have explained, the verse taken by itself does not support the notion of a virgin birth. Much more hangs on Matthew's twice-repeated claim that Jesus is 'from the Holy Spirit'. Yet other biblical material, and particularly passages in Paul and John, would encourage us to interpret that phrase figuratively, rather than literally.

This means that the New Testament gives no clear support for the doctrine of the virgin birth. It is an invention of theologians beyond the New Testament period. Of course, both Matthew and Luke have often been called upon to support it, but only if we approach their stories thinking it must be there will we find it. If we take away the lens of that doctrine, and look at their texts with an open mind, we begin to see a different and a much larger miracle.

Matthew and Luke agree that Joseph was not Jesus' natural father. Matthew makes that quite plain. Luke implies it in Mary's annunciation scene, and then settles the matter when he eventually gives Jesus' genealogy, and begins it with the words, 'He was the son (*as was thought*) of Joseph' (Luke 3.23, my italics). Mark makes no mention of Joseph, and writes his Gospel as if he was not there. Twice John has characters refer to Jesus as 'the son of Joseph' (John 1.45; 6.42), and yet it is he who brings closest to the surface the understanding that Jesus was illegitimate.

All four Gospel writers seem to know of the claim of Jesus' illegitimacy. Too often that claim is summarily dismissed as the late invention of Jesus' Jewish opponents. That is partly because of a work by a Christian theologian called Origen, his *Against Celsus*, written in the middle of the third century. In arguing against Celsus, Origen quotes his opponent or refers to his opinions. Among those is the idea that Mary was seduced by a soldier called Panthera, and was then 'driven out by the carpenter to whom she was betrothed, since she was convicted of adultery'. According to Origen, Celsus did not invent that story, but drew it from an unnamed Jewish source. That legend, with all its particular detail, was no doubt some time in the making, and of course has little or no historical credibility. Stories have a habit of gathering detail to themselves, as over time people repeat them and fill in the gaps. Nevertheless, this much remains true: Mark leaves the question of Jesus' illegitimacy open, but pays it hardly any heed; John brings it to the surface, and does not refute it; both Matthew and Luke seem to accept it.

It may be that John himself believed that Joseph was Jesus' biological father. It is not clear what he thought, but that is itself of great significance. No one in the New Testament has a higher view of Jesus, a more exalted notion of his status, of his divinity, than John. Yet how Jesus was conceived, and who his natural father was, is of no interest to him, and makes no difference. 'In the beginning was the Word, and the Word was with God, and the Word was God' (John 1.1). That is all that matters. 'The Father and I are one,' he has Jesus say (10.30). That is what is important.

Matthew and Luke do not argue for a virgin birth, nor do they think Joseph was Jesus' father. Presumably, therefore, they both believed Jesus was illegitimate. Luke either thought that was of no importance, like John and Mark, or else he was careful to hide his belief beneath the surface of his narrative, fearing what opponents of the Church might do with it. Matthew was less cautious, and he dwells for a few moments on the disgrace that illegitimacy might bring in its wake. But he goes on to argue that in Jesus' case that disgrace is turned all to good by the work of the Holy Spirit.

What are we to make of this? Have we shown that the doctrine of the virgin birth is built on sand? Not necessarily. All we have done is argue that its foundations are not to be found ready laid in the New Testament. That does not of itself mean the foundations are unsound. The Wisdom and Spirit of God did not go on permanent leave after the New Testament documents were completed. As far as we know, Justin Martyr, who lived c.110–166 CE, was the first person to claim in so many words that Mary conceived Jesus without sexual intercourse, and Irenaeus (c.120–202) the first to insist that the virgin birth was an essential part of Christian teaching. Perhaps they were right. After all, a very great many Christians still agree with them.

The question we need to address is this: whenever and however the doctrine of the virgin birth came into being, what does it imply about sex, about women, about the mission of the Church, about Jesus, and about God and his ways of working? And when we have clarified the implications, do we like what we see?

Like the story of Jesus' illegitimacy, the tale of Mary's virgin birth was soon elaborated. In the second half of the second century the claim came to be made that Mary remained a virgin all her life, that Joseph was an aged widower who never had sexual relations with her, and that the brothers of Jesus referred to in the New Testament were stepbrothers from Joseph's first marriage. Around the same time, or even earlier, others made the birth of Jesus entirely painless. In their version of the story, Mary does not have to endure labour: Jesus simply 'appears' as a small child when Mary and Joseph are alone, to Mary's amazement and Joseph's initial bewilderment. (We are getting close here to the familiar nativity play, where Mary suddenly produces a doll from beneath her cloak, or else a real baby is slipped onto the platform and put as inconspicuously as possible into the crib.) Then came the assertions of Mary's immaculate conception, whereby she escaped the detritus of 'original sin' passed on through sexual intercourse, the belief in her assumption into heaven, and her coronation as the Queen of Heaven. In Chester Cathedral we have one of the finest set of medieval choir stalls in the country. They were carved in the late fourteenth century for the Benedictine monks, whose monastery the church was, until later Henry VIII dissolved it and turned it into a cathedral. The most elaborate of the bench ends belongs to what was once the Abbot's stall, now the Dean's. It shows a small 'tree of Jesse' and portrays a series of figures rising out of Jesse lying horizontal at the bottom. Those figures begin, of course, with David, and we might expect them to end with Jesus as his most illustrious descendant. But they do not. As our eye moves up the scene, it stops at Mary. There she is, flanked by God the Father and God the Son, and with the dove of the Holy Spirit above her head. The Holy Trinity is attending to her coronation, and the Father and the Son are placing the crown upon her head!

That bench end could not depict more clearly Mary's acceptance into the godhead. In some parts of the Church she has been turned into a goddess in all but name. People pray to her, and surround her with language and ritual befitting a goddess. In a religion where God is invariably portrayed as male and sometimes as intolerably macho, Mary's elevation might be thought a very good thing indeed. We might say with relief that she has brought some much-needed femininity into the Christian understanding of the divine.

That may be so, but the price we have had to pay is very high. With the Queen of Heaven blocking our view, we have lost sight entirely of the Gospel narratives and the young Jewish girl who inhabits their pages. Her humanity, her vulnerability, her courage, her faith are no longer to be seen. And we find ourselves suggesting that to be free of sin, to remain pure and unsullied, a woman must have nothing at all to do with sex. The notion of sex as polluting has bedevilled the Church's teaching about relationships for almost its entire existence and, alas, it still does. There is but one Christian denomination in this country which has been able to give a lead to our society in its thinking about sexual matters, and that is the Society of Friends, with their remarkable *Towards a Quaker View of Sex*, published in 1963. That was a groundbreaking study and ahead of its times. As for the rest of us, the best of our secular thinkers, in their clarity, common sense and compassion, still too often find themselves having to drag us kicking and screaming to a place where we can face realities. The current debate in the Church about homosexuality is a case in point.

The view that sex is somehow polluting, and that Mary, in order to remain sinless, had to keep free of it, is both pathological and an insult to God. It flies in the face of reality, and turns its back on the Creator. It denies the goodness, the very-goodness of sex within a loving relationship, as an expression of love and as a genuine making of love. The phrase 'making love' is sometimes used too casually, but it can carry the great truth that sexual intercourse can and does *create* a profound intimacy that goes far beyond the physical union, and is so significant in establishing and deepening commitment, that the non-consummation of a marriage is regarded as grounds for divorce or annulment. And sex also belongs to the way God made us. Are we going to argue God made a fundamental mistake, or else resort to the miserable doctrine of the Fall and, with an absurd, tragic twisting of the sparkling tale of the Garden of Eden in Genesis, say that sex belongs to our fallen nature?

If the doctrine of the virgin birth is not good for sex, it is not good for women, either. Most organized religions have not been good news for women. Though their founders may have conveyed a vision of human society that was and still is profoundly liberating for women, their male followers have quickly seen to it that that vision has been lost sight of, and have twisted their founders' teachings to keep women under their authority. Within Christianity those denominations and individual churches which have most highly exalted Mary have been and still are the ones which find it most difficult to place women in public positions of authority. That might seem strange, until we recall the Mary they have created, and what they do with her image. They have both emphasized Mary's 'humility' and also put her on a towering pedestal, and then effectively told the women among their members that they must be like her. Like this Mary, they must be obedient, submissive to male authority; they must not question, nor resist, nor attempt to run things their way; if they see things differently, they must keep their mouths shut; they must learn to play men's games, and learn them so well that they will themselves be outraged if anyone suggests fundamental change. They must, if they are to fulfil their womanhood, become mothers (that effectively excludes countless women, of course), while extolling perpetual virginity as the ideal state. Thus these churches offer women a role model which is on the one hand quite impossible, so setting them up for failure, and on the other only attainable if they are subservient to men, so setting them up for all kinds of abuse.

I am aware, of course, of the many Christians who would wholeheartedly agree with this comment of L. N. Bell's about Jesus:

> If He was not virgin-born, then His mother was a promiscuous and dishonest woman and He was an illegitimate son. If He was not virgin-born, then He himself was deluded and the entire structure of His Person and Work is undermined and we become of all men most miserable.
>
> (quoted by H. A. Hanke in *The Validity of the Virgin Birth*, 1963, p. 107)

Such a statement, apart from its thinly veiled misogyny, is, however, most curious. As we have discovered, none of the New Testament writers need belief in the virgin birth to make their claims about Jesus. John can describe Thomas, confronted with the risen Jesus, crying out, 'My Lord and my God!' without having any birth narratives in his Gospel at all. It was the encounter with the risen Jesus, not any notion about the manner of his conception, that compelled his followers to see and proclaim him as the one who put God's feet on this earth, and withdrew the veil from the face of heaven.

In truth, I believe the doctrine of the virgin birth is bad, not good news for Jesus. In a powerful article in the collection edited by George Brooke, *The Birth of Jesus* (2004), Arthur Peacocke, who was both a scientist trained in physical biochemistry and a theologian, starts asking questions about Jesus' chromosomes, DNA and genetic inheritance. You only have to pose such questions to realize that the virgin birth makes it impossible to believe Jesus of Nazareth was a human being. It does not turn him into a God, but into a freak, and its understanding of God is positively alarming. As Peacocke says, rather more politely,

> the present understanding of the biology of reproduction and of heredity reveals the doctrine of the virginal conception to be postulating an extraordinary, almost magical, divine act of suddenly bringing into existence a complex biological entity. All the evidence is that is *not* how God has created and is creating – certainly not the God whose mode of being and becoming it is possible to believe in today. (*The Birth of Jesus*, p. 65)

That comment makes plain that the virgin birth is not only bad news for sex, women and Jesus, but for the mission of the Church and for God himself. It is ironical that some of those who insist that Christians must believe in the virgin birth in order to be Christian also place the greatest stress upon the mission of the Church, and put the most energy and time into promoting it. As Peacocke suggests, what they end up doing is telling a story of God which is impossible for most people to accept. They reduce the Christian faith, if they are not careful, to the proverbial ten impossible things to believe before breakfast. Most people in this country hardly give the Christian faith a thought. There are many reasons for that, but one is that they think we insist on calling true what they see as plainly silly.

But it is God I am most concerned about. The virgin birth presents us with a God who chooses to bypass or ignore the ways of his creation, and that is not the God I know myself, nor the one I wish to proclaim. Instead I keep stumbling across my God as the mystery within and beyond the ordinary, the one who turns the ordinary into the extraordinary, who leads us through, not round it into the mystery of his presence. Suddenly, with our feet still firmly rooted, we find ourselves on holy ground. That is how it is with Moses in the story of the burning bush, or with Peter, James and John in the story of the transfiguration. That is how it is with us, also. As I say in my reflection 'Waiting for God', 'God is all about us in the wild skies, the clouds unravelled by the wind . . . in the kindness of strangers, in acts of unexpected courtesy . . . in the delight of small children, and the quiet courage of the old; in the banter of hospital wards.'

There is more to say, however, about this God. Nowhere is God more plainly revealed than in situations where good is brought out of evil or, to use a line from another of my reflections, where 'disgrace is turned quite all to grace'. And that is why I believe the story of an illegitimate Jesus, even the story of a raped Mary, is such good news for all of us. For see what God does with such beginnings! Out of humiliation and violence he brings the greatest good the world has ever seen! He enters into the dark not just of a young girl's womb, but into the deeper darkness of her abuse and terror, and into the dark of the fears and prejudice surrounding her, to turn it all into dazzling light! And if he does that once, he can do it again, turn the darkness of our own pain into light. Of course, he *does* do it again, at the end of the Gospels' story of Jesus. Out of the even more terrible humiliation, violence and hurt of crucifixion, he brings the highest hope and reveals the eternal triumph of Love. When we look into the face of the crucified Jesus, we find ourselves looking into the face of God, and we know God is not defeated, nor ever can be. Behind the ugly brutality of the cross and its dark, we catch the dawn of resurrection.

Of all the Gospels, Matthew's most clearly tells the wonderful tale of 'disgrace turned quite all to grace', for he is the one who both begins and ends his Gospel with that theme. But it is Luke, perhaps, who leaves us with the most profound, the most enduring image of God from these stories of a child's birth. It is not only standing beneath a cross that we find ourselves face to face with God. The same happens when we kneel beside a manger. That is why we celebrate Christmas with such gusto, and why some people who cannot handle our God at other times of year are strangely drawn towards him then. For at Christmas we all find ourselves with a God who does not threaten or condemn, but a God (wonder of wonders!) we can hold in our arms; a God who does not wish to be left out in the cold and needs the warmth of our hospitality and care; a